food of my friends

the best meals in town

Other books by Judith Shepard
SEASCAPES

judith shepard

food of my friends
the best meals in town

the permanent press
sagaponack, n.y. 11962

Library of Congress Number: 81-81400
International Standard Book Number: 0-932966-17-9
Manufactured in the United States of America
THE PERMANENT PRESS
Sagaponack NY 11962

thanks

For many, many years, whenever family or friends served me a dish that I particularly liked, I invariably asked for the recipe, then prepared it at home the very next day. Living out in the Hamptons, my husband and I found that we were sharing many communal meals and that good dishes were showing up constantly. One day, as we were discussing where we should go out to eat, he remarked that he was spoiled. Our home and the homes of our friends serve "the best meals in town," he said. That is how this book came to be written and it is to all those superb cooks that it is dedicated, as well as to my husband and children who sampled all of the recipes.

I want to give special thanks to my friends Mary Cummings who edited this book, and therefore helped me sleep much more soundly, and to Karen Sukoneck who designed such a pretty cover.

contents

foreword

I have just been browsing through the cookbook department of a large and popular bookstore wondering why on earth I am writing a cookbook. There is such a huge and dazzling selection of them. Many are tempting to me, even though I have more of my own than I could possibly use. I guess that is my answer right there. I am a collector of cookbooks; I always have been, and it looks as if I always will be. Furthermore, there seem to be others out there just like me, both men and women. That's why cookbooks proliferate like the proverbial rabbit.

Of course I collect recipes too, cutting them from magazines and newspapers now, just as I did when I was in the seventh grade and starting my first home economics class. I must have enough to feed a small army with nary a repeat.

I like to cook. I seem to meditate upon a great many things while chopping, stir frying, and mixing. My children wonder grumpily why I can't cook "like other mothers do," and why they never seem to have the same dish twice—a slight exaggeration expressed in pique, frustration or, sometimes, in a teasing affectionate way.

I also like to eat. I am not considered particularly gluttonous, but for me one of life's greatest pleasures comes when I sit down to a fine meal, especially if I am truly hungry and not just eating out of habit.

It's nice to cook for family and friends. In a way, it's a gift I am offering them, and good food not only nourishes the body, it pleasures the soul.

Perhaps beneath all of these rationalizations for indulging my mania for cookbooks and recipes, there is something deep in my genetic makeup which prompts me to follow the practice of centuries. Originally a matter of survival, it now involves much more than mere nourishment. I know myself as a wife, mother, and hostess who likes to cook for and feed those she cares about.

introduction

I have been interested in good nutrition and healthy preparation of food since the day, sixteen years ago, when I walked into a Chicago bookstore and picked up a book by Gaylord Hauser. Until that time, good nutrition meant to me only what most seventh graders learn in home economics class: eight glasses of milk a day, one or more servings of meat and eggs, plenty of fruit and green, leafy vegetables, etcetera, etcetera. I was later surprised to discover that doctors in medical school learn very little more than that.

At that time, my ex-husband and I were on a ten-month tour of the play, *Who's Afraid of Virginia Woolf,* covering twenty-eight cities. With us were our children, Aaron, Liza, and Caleb, all under six. It was a strenuous time—performing, packing, unpacking, and traveling from city to city with three little children. Mid-tour, when we reached Chicago, everyone was feeling the strain and fatigue. Browsing through Mr. Hauser's book, I became intrigued with his message—that it is possible to enjoy better health, more energy, and even a calmer state of mind with the right foods and the right preparation.

I bought the book, and since in each town we usually had a small kitchen, I began to experiment, changing my approach, my menus, and our lives. We did, indeed, begin to feel better. We had more energy, less fatigue, and experienced a greater sense of well-being. As a bonus, eating and cooking were more fun, more like creative endeavors.

From then on, I began to read what others said on the subject. I was especially impressed with Adele Davis's proposition that "you are what you eat." It seemed so eminently sensible. Of course, there are always detractors, many of them from the professional community. But in the end, the way you feel seems to be the best and most reliable guide. What all this seemed to offer me was some kind of control over my own body. Nowadays, they call it preventive medicine. I believe there is no doubt that what you put in your body directly affects your physical, mental, and emotional well-being. So it is well worth your while to *observe* what you ingest.

It has been a matter of interest and curiosity to me that various people concerned about health and nutrition have seen their ideas derided and scorned over the years by both professional people and those involved in the food industry. Many have been labeled charlatans and quacks. Over the years, looking through my present husband's medical journals, I have begun to notice small changes. Ideas that once were derided are now given second thoughts and serious attention. I understand that some medical schools are even beginning to offer more comprehensive courses on nutrition.

Finally, after attempting to sort out the volumes of often contradictory information telling me what I should and shouldn't do, I decided to follow my own intuition and common sense. Too much conflicting advice can be paralyzing. So I try to be aware of what feels best. With that in mind, I offer some simple guidelines that have helped me sort through the enormous variety of choices encountered as I continue the lifelong process of feeding family and friends.

notes and guidelines

notes and guidelines

The following practices have evolved for me over a number of years. Along with the guidelines, I want to add a small disclaimer. I am not a "purist." I believe in flexibility. There are recipes in this book that do not adhere to the principles I have set down. I know that Anchovy Spaghetti has great quantities of butter and salt and that Mrs. Knudson's Coffeecake calls for white sugar and flour. Since these recipes have been collected over a long period of time, there are inconsistencies. I can make my peace with the occasional breach because I am always aware of ingredients and preparation and try to make sure that I do not use recipes that violate my principles too often. Certain dishes are included because they just taste very good, and I tell myself—everything in moderation, including moderation.

1. Shopping

Shop for quality. That's the first rule of thumb. I don't like to try and disguise inferior products or produce. I like to buy the best I can afford without being needlessly extravagant. At one time I loved to try and cut corners by following all those weekly menus printed in homemaking magazines, feeling that I was "stretching my dollar." Now I am appalled at the meals I served and hope I have found better ways to be economical.

I would rather have one serving of good fresh fish twice a month than two servings of mediocre fish twice a week. I am also willing to settle for smaller portions. That's one way to cut costs.

I rarely use canned or frozen vegetables and fruit. Fresh ones are healthier. They taste better. They look better. If you buy in season, you'll find it's a practical way to shop. (Canned tomatoes, paste and puree are the exceptions, but if you can preserve your own, that's even nicer.) What all this means is that you must find a butcher, a fishmonger and a greengrocer whom you can trust, who want to sell you good quality foods without depleting your pocketbook. It's almost like interviewing for a family doctor. In both cases, it's worth it.

I never buy "Instant" anything. You know three things about it: it's going to cost you more; it usually tastes awful, and it can't be as nutritious as the real thing.

2. Meats

I am not a strict vegetarian, but in our family we eat very little red meat, sticking to fish and poultry, and probably eating them only two to three times a week. We might have meat twice a month. I believe that in this country we consume far too much meat. Some people eat bacon and sausage for breakfast, hamburgers for lunch, and then settle down to pork chops for dinner. Think of those food bills! Besides, it can be dangerous to your health. Animals raised today are fed commercial feed containing perservatives, hormones, antibiotics, and other dietary supplements. These additives are concentrated in the animal's tissues and passed on to us. The argument is constantly made that the amounts are miniscule, but it still makes me nervous. Suppose it all adds up—like back taxes? I don't like experimenting on my body.

As far as protein needs go, my husband loves to tell the story of an 84-year-old yogi named Swami Bua. He was asked how he remained in such superb shape on a diet of fruits and nuts.

"Where do you get your protein?" my husband inquired.

"Look at the elephant," Swami Bua answered, his eyes twinkling, "the largest mass of protein on earth. He manufactures everything he needs by eating grass, leaves and twigs."

One last item! I thought it would be terribly difficult cutting down on meat. It wasn't at all.

3.   Additives

I buy nothing that contains preservatives, artificial flavors, dyes, calcium proprionate, nitrates, nitrites, sodium benzoate, dough conditioners (which may contain sodium stearoyl-2-lactylate, mono and diglycerides, ethoxylated mono and diglycerides, succinylated mono glycerides). I don't buy any breads with the pleasant sounding "yeast nutrients" listed among the ingredients, because that's really ammonium chloride and potassium bromate. I used to think that dough conditioners and yeast nutrients were harmless ingredients. Now I feel as though I'm being tricked. Label reading should be done with a healthy dose of cynicism. For those of you who, like me, don't remember much of your chemistry and are having trouble deciphering the labels, here is my husband's formula: when in doubt, don't buy anything containing an ingredient which is not a familiar foodstuff.

I would also advise you to scrutinize all labels carefully. Nothing makes me angrier than to see a product labeled "all natural" or "no preservatives" in big letters and then to find, in tiny letters on the back, an ingredient that contradicts that claim.

4.   Butter, Oils and Margerine

After studying all the pros and cons, I have opted for butter over margarine. It simply has many fewer additives. Since it is a saturated fat, I try to use it sparingly. I have switched to sweet rather than salted butter. Salt masks rancidity and sweet butter seems fresher. It's probably worthwhile to reduce salt intake anyway.

If I can substitute vegetable oils for butter, so much the better. I use only cold-pressed, poly-unsaturated ones. All others are hydrogenated, which means they contain preservatives to prolong their shelf life, and valuable nutrients are lost.

My favorite cooking oil is a cold-pressed, poly-unsaturated safflower oil because it seems so light. I use olive oil for some dishes and salads and, occasionally, walnut or sesame oil. Whatever you buy, be careful with margarines and oils that contain cottonseed oil. Since cotton is not considered an edible crop, it is often heavily sprayed with pesticides that make their way into the products sold at the grocer's.

5. Sweeteners

I don't use white sugar. It has been processed and does nothing for you. On the other hand, it does a lot against you, contributing to obesity, tooth decay, and the depletion of B vitamins. The amount of sugar added to packaged foods staggers the imagination; you'd be surprised where food manufacturers have sneaked it in.

The best sugar substitutes are unsulphured molasses, honey, and maple syrup. If I need sugar for something, I use raw sugar. There is a certain amount of controversy surrounding it, but raw sugar may contain some of the original nutrients. No chemical has been added to make it "anti-caking" and it has not been exposed to the whitening process. It is another ingredient, like butter, that I try to use sparingly.

6. Flour

Most of the time I try to use stone-ground, unrefined whole wheat flour, especially for thickening and for making sauces, breads and muffins. I must admit that in making desserts I usually use an unbleached white flour. Without it, the results are a little too heavy for me. Some of my friends say they use half unbleached white flour and half whole wheat, sift it together, and get good results.

7. Rice

I have grown increasingly fond of brown rice and use it frequently. It's inexpensive and can be prepared in a variety of ways. It contains all the natural nutrients, while white rice loses many of them in the processing. When I do use white rice, I choose a converted brand which contains more vitamins than the non-converted ones.

8. Milk, Cream, and Yogurt

I substitute dry skim milk for fresh milk in all my cooking. It's better for you, contains less fat, is cheaper, and nobody can tell the difference. For drinking, I mix half fresh milk with half dry skim milk. Unfortunately, I love cream. Since I use dry milk for practically everything, I indulge myself once in a while.

I make my own yogurt and use it as a substitution whenever any recipe calls for sour cream. By making it myself, again using dry skim milk, I can have yogurt that is not only nutritious but much less fattening and cheaper than what the supermarket offers.

9. Breakfast Cereals

I have always resisted buying all those famous American breakfast cereals, no matter how many ads promoted them and no matter how much my children clamored for them after watching TV. I buy cereals from the health food stores, make my own dry cereal mixes, or choose one from the small selection of dry cereals without preservatives at the supermarket. I read all labels very carefully. I add untoasted wheat germ, which is extremely nutritious, to all cereals. Incidentally, dry, untoasted wheat germ should be kept in the refrigerator or it will soon spoil and taste rancid.

10. Salt

Salt is a natural ingredient in all foods. By adding more in the cooking process and more at the table, we are really overdosing on salt. Most supermarket salt has many additives, including aluminum compounds and other agents which make it pour easier. This little convenience I can certainly do without. I purchase vegetable salts and unrefined sea salt, rich in minerals and iodine, in the health food store and try to practice moderation. In most of the recipes, I have omitted specific amounts for both salt and pepper, preferring to allow you to follow your own taste buds or inclination to cut down on either ingredient.

11. Breads

It's very hard to find a bread without calcium proprionate or some other kind of additive or preservative in it, but it can be done. Health food stores and local bakeries are often good sources. Fortunately, my husband bakes bread and that's a big help.

12. Health Food Stores

We have good health food stores out here in the Hamptons. Some of the things I buy there are dried fruits because they have not been preserved with sulfur dioxide, seeds and nuts because they are unroasted and unsalted (making them less fattening and more digestible), and bouillon cubes (since the bouillon cubes sold in supermarkets are practically solid chemicals). I purchase other interesting foods there including tamari (a soy sauce without a preservative), sprouts, seeds, tofu (made from soybean curd), tahini (a sesame seed butter), wheat berries, a variety of honeys and herbal teas, hotdogs made without nitrates, and many more intriguing items. I realize that there are some health food stores that have exorbitantly high prices and inferior products; in this respect it is just like any other business. But if you can shop around until you find a good one, or a food co-op, you will be doing yourself a favor. Be aware, however, that since these items are not loaded with chemicals, many of them must be refrigerated, while others do not have a very long shelf life. It's a small price to pay for your health, don't you think?

13. Cooking Methods

I almost always short-cook vegetables or steam them, using very little water. I think that everyone knows by now that vitamins go down the drain with the water, so the less used, the better. I rarely deep fry, although once in a while I make tempura. I don't think that all those oil-drenched foods can be good for either your health or your weight. I don't even pan fry very often, preferring to saute, steam, or bake. I have also thrown away all my aluminum pots and pans. Do you know that it is illegal to sell them in some European countries? Aluminum is a soft metal, can dissolve during cooking, and be ingested. I use only heavy cast iron, stainless steel, enamel or clay pots.

14. Quantity

Most of the recipes in this book feed four to six people.

15. A Last Thought: Time

One of the biggest and most persuasive criticisms of this way of cooking is that it takes more time. That is absolutely true. I can put some potatoes in the oven, open up a box of frozen vegetables, and a bag of dinner rolls, chop some lettuce and sprinkle it with prepared dressing, put a steak on the broiler, thaw a frozen chocolate cake and—presto—I have a meal that the kids are guaranteed to love. However, it's not for me. I just don't feel good about cooking this way. As I'm peeling, chopping and stir frying, I know it's worth it. It's not only tastier, it's healthier. After all, being sick takes time too and it can be expensive and painful as well.

If you like to cook, it helps. It can be as rewarding creatively as painting a picture or composing a song. To be an artist in the kitchen doesn't mean you have to be a preparer of exotic, complicated, and expensive dishes. It can mean simply that you take great pleasure in what you are doing and do it all with a point of view.

appetizers

appetizers

The problem with appetizers is that we eat too many of them. They are intended to "whet the appetite" and prepare us for the feast to come. Instead, we stuff ourselves gluttonously and then moan and groan when the first course appears. I have finally realized that I enjoy my meals a great deal more if I don't overindulge. Here, then, are a few good recipes. The less served, the better.

My friend, Jane Wilson, has a catering service in New York called "The Party Box." She is a marvelously creative cook who puts meals together like an artist mixing her paints. Once, at a local food stand, some beautiful cauliflower so entranced her that she decided to concoct an all white dinner, which turned out splendidly, as usual. She has helped me to explore the color and textures of food. This is a snack which she brought back from Japan.

jane's japanese peanuts

Crystallized ginger (about 6 pieces, each the size of a quarter)
1   6½-oz. can salted peanuts

1. Cut the ginger into small pieces.
2. Mix the ginger with the peanuts and serve.
     Simple!!

We have two good friends, Florence and Jerry Grey. Florence is a fashion illustrator and Jerry is an engineer and a solar-energy consultant. They both have boundless energy, it seems, and entertain frequently and very well, always preparing the dinner together. I often wonder how they fit everything into their busy schedule with such apparent ease. I suspect they're both very organized, something more difficult to copy than their recipes.

florence's seviche

2   small fish fillets (flounder, weakfish, etc.)
2 or 3 limes
1/2 lb. scallops
Chinese Hot Pepper and Garlic Sauce (This can be found in Chinese stores, or in Chinese sections of certain markets. It should be used sparingly, to taste. If you can't find it, use some hot chilis and garlic, also sparingly.)

1. Cut the fillets into bite-size pieces.
2. Squeeze two limes.
3. Mix fillet pieces with the scallops and pour the lime juice over fish. The juice should cover the fish; if there is not enough use the third lime.
4. Marinate (soak) for at least three hours, preferably overnight.
5. When you are ready to serve the seviche, add ¼ tsp. of the Chinese sauce, stir well and test for spiciness. Add more sauce if you like it hotter.

florence's sardine dip

2　cans sardines (4½-oz. each)
1　small onion, minced
2　tsp. dry mustard
1　tbsp. lemon juice
1/2 cup yogurt
Chopped parsley for garnish

1. Drain oil from sardines and mash in small bowl.
2. Add onion to sardines.
3. Mix mustard and lemon juice with yogurt.
4. Add yogurt mixture to sardines and mix thoroughly.
5. Garnish with chopped parsley.

One evening we were invited for dinner at our cousin Cynthia's house. We already had plans for later in the evening, so she urged us to come just for drinks and a first course. She explained that a friend, who had a cooking school in New York, would be there. When we arrived, everyone was busily following her friend's instructions. The first course was a quiche which was so good and so easy to make that I have included it as a last-minute addition. It was served as an hors d'oeuvre, but it might easily be included as part of the main dinner.

easy quiche

1　10-inch pie shell
3　medium tomatoes
2　tbsp. oil
1　tbsp. vinegar
Salt and pepper, to taste
2　tbsp. Dijon type mustard
1/2 lb. Danish Fontina cheese, sliced
1/4 cup grated Parmesan cheese

1. Bake pie shell until done.
2. While pie shell is baking, slice tomatoes and marinate in the oil, vinegar, salt, and pepper.
3. Cool pie shell and spread with mustard.
4. Place the sliced and drained tomatoes on top of the mustard.
5. Place Fontina over the tomatoes.
6. Sprinkle with grated Parmesan and bake in a 350-degree oven until cheese has melted.

Bernice Hunt seems to do all things well. Along with having raised a family, she is also a writer, an editor, and a superb cook. She is aided and abetted in all this by her husband, Morton, also a writer and a gardener who manages to grow lovely vegetables without using either herbicides or pesticides. Bernice has written an excellent book called *The Bread Book* for which Morton tested the recipes. They make good partners and the meals that they serve are always both simple and elegant.

bernice's anchovy spread

4   tbsp. butter, softened
4   oz. cream cheese, softened
5   tbsp. anchovy paste
1   tbsp. parsley, chopped

1. Blend the butter, cream cheese and paste into a smooth mixture, suitable for spreading.
2. Garnish with chopped parsley.
3. Serve with crackers.

This is an appetizer that I copied from a restaurant in San Francisco years ago. I don't make it as much now because I don't like all the preservatives in bacon, and I prefer not to deep fry. However, it's quite exotic and if it is accompanied by the kind of rum punches the restaurant served, you might even forget all that.

rumaki

6   pieces of bacon (some stores carry bacon without preservatives.)
1/4 pound chicken livers
Garlic salt, to taste
1   8-oz. can water chestnuts
Corn or safflower oil for deep frying

1. Cut bacon into two-inch pieces.
2. Cut chicken livers into small bite-sized

pieces, removing any membranes.
3. Sprinkle liver with garlic salt.
4. Alternate bacon, liver, and water chestnuts on small skewers.
5. Bring oil to boil in a deep fryer or a heavy, deep saucepan.
6. Deep fry, a few at a time, making sure the bacon is thoroughly cooked.
7. Drain and serve warm.

We have two lovely and special friends named Bill and Gay Tarlo. Bill is a retired English barrister and Gay is pure New England. They entertain beautifully in a house filled with shining silver, lovely antiques, and a profusion of flowers. Gay has a great eye for color and style. Bill loves to cook and has a great eye, period—with a perennially mischievous twinkle. For years he has been promising me his curry recipe for which he is famous, but I just can't seem to pry it away. However, he did call to donate these two party appetizers.

bill's basic ham sauce

1/3 cup cream
1/3 cup chutney
1/3 cup mustard sauce. (See last chapter for recipe.)

1. Blend all ingredients in a blender to make a smooth sauce.
2. Serve on buttered, thin sandwich bread with thin slices of ham.

bill's tuna dip

1   cup of Bill's basic ham sauce
1   cup sour cream
1   large can tuna (6½-oz.), drained
1   tsp. curry powder
1/4 tsp. red pepper flakes

1. Blend all ingredients and serve with raw vegetables and/or crackers.

The next three recipes have evolved over the years. I can't credit any particular person. They are probably "remembrances of things past," embellished and made my own. There are many versions of guacamole, I know, but this one seems consistently good.

salmon spread

1   8-oz. can salmon
1   8-oz. package of softened cream cheese
2   tbsp. dill weed or 4 tbsp. of fresh dill, minced.
Salt and pepper

1. Drain salmon and chop *very thoroughly*.
2. Mix the cream cheese and salmon.
3. Add the dill and salt and pepper to taste and mix well.

guacamole

2 ripe avocados
1 small, ripe tomato
1 small onion, minced
1 tsp. olive oil
Juice of 2 lemons
Salt to taste
1 chili pepper, minced, or 2 tsp. chili powder (more for spicier version)

1. Skin avocados and mash the pulp thoroughly.
2. Skin tomato, chop into small pieces, and add to avocado.
3. Mince onion and add to avocado mixture.
4. Add olive oil and stir.
5. Add lemon juice and salt to taste; stir again.
6. Add chili pepper or powder; use more if you like it hotter.
7. Stir, chill, and serve with crackers, corn chips or celery.

anchovy-tuna spread

1 2-oz. can anchovies
4 tbsp. tuna fish, drained and chopped
2 hard-boiled eggs, chopped fine
1 small tomato, chopped
1/2 sweet pepper, chopped fine
2 tbsp. onion, minced
1 or 2 sweet pickles, minced
Black pepper, to taste
1/2 cup mayonnaise
3 tbsp. catsup
Parsley, for garnish

1. Drain anchovies well and chop into very small pieces.
2. Add tuna and mix well.
3. Add eggs, tomato, onion, sweet pepper, pickles, black pepper and mix.
4. Mix mayonnaise with catsup and add to mixture, stirring well. (For creamier consistency, add more mayonnaise.)
5. Decorate with parsley and serve with melba toast.

My mother is pretty, very youthful looking, and known for her thoughtfulness. She has been making cheese balls for years. At Christmas, she wraps them in cellophane, ties them with a bow, and hands them out to friends who drop by. Since exotic cheeses are so expensive, this is a nice, inexpensive way to economize.

mother's christmas cheese ball

1/2 cup chopped walnuts
4   oz. blue cheese, softened
8   oz. package cream cheese, softened
1   tbsp. pimento, finely chopped
1   tbsp. green pepper, finely chopped
Salt and pepper, to taste

1. Heat oven to 350 degrees and toast walnuts on a baking sheet for about 8 minutes, being careful not to burn them.
2. Blend softened blue cheese, cream cheese, pimento, and green pepper in a blender, or by hand.
3. Add a dash of salt and pepper.
4. Shape into a ball and chill until firm.
5. Roll cheese ball in the toasted walnuts.
6. Serve cold with crackers.

These are two dips for dunking. I like to serve them with whatever vegetables are in season, such as broccoli, celery, radishes, mushrooms, zucchini, string beans, cauliflower, etc.

tarragon dip

3/4 cup yogurt
1/4 cup cottage cheese
Juice from one clove garlic
1   tbsp. lemon juice
1   tbsp. tarragon

1. Mix all ingredients well and serve with vegetables.

curry dip

1   cup yogurt
Juice from 1 clove garlic
1   tbsp. lemon juice
1   tsp. minced onion
1   tbsp. curry powder
2   tbsp. sesame seeds

1. Mix all ingredients.
2. Sprinkle with sesame seeds.

Dorothy Friedman seems to have a special way with vegetables. I asked her husband, Gene, why he thought her dishes were so distinctive. He said that she tastes and seasons a great deal as she's cooking. Dorothy volunteered another secret—substitution. In other words, if she usually makes potatoes au gratin, but happens to see some nice turnips at the grocery, she asks herself, "Why not turnips au gratin?" Why not indeed! I have many of her recipes in the section on vegetables, but here is one of her appetizers.

dorothy's eggplant

1   medium eggplant
1   small onion, minced
1   small green pepper, minced
2   tbsp. olive oil
Juice of two lemons
1   clove of garlic, pressed
Cayenne pepper, to taste
Salt, to taste
1   tbsp. parsley, minced

1. Pierce the eggplant with a fork in a few places and bake in a 350-degree oven until done, about one hour.
2. Peel eggplant, chop into small pieces, and let drain in a colander.
3. Add minced onion and green pepper to eggplant.
4. Toss eggplant mixture with olive oil.
5. Add lemon juice and stir.
6. Add cayenne pepper to taste. (Dorothy makes hers quite spicy and I prefer it to a milder version.)
7. Sprinkle parsley on top.
8. Chill and serve with crackers.

soups

soups

Adele Davis said that the best way to make soup was to save all your leftovers for a week—vegetable parings, broths, even scraps from your plate, if you're not too squeamish. Then she recommended that everything be boiled vigorously in a pot of water for fifteen minutes, strained and allowed to sit overnight. In the morning you have a vitamin-enriched broth from which to make your soup. I have tried her method, but find that often I like to start from scratch. My husband prefers her way and loves to throw in "everything but the kitchen sink." To me, they usually taste very good, but the children invariably scream, "Oh, no, not one of Dad's soups again!" Whatever method you choose, the two basic requirements are a large soup pot so things don't become crowded and, for most recipes, plenty of time for long, leisurely cooking. Remember that a fine meal can consist of soup, salad, bread and a piece of fruit for dessert—nothing fancier.

My son Caleb is eighteen now but has been making this soup since he was about twelve years old. He has always had a great deal of enthusiasm for many things and cooking is no exception. He's a happy cook. Maybe that's a secret ingredient. I think this started out as one of my recipes, but he took it over, gradually adding his own embellishments.

caleb's clam chowder

1½ cups chopped onions
4   good-sized potatoes, peeled and diced
1   pint clam juice
1/2 tsp. salt
1/4 tsp. pepper
2   cans minced clams with juice, or a comparable amount of fresh, cooked clams
1   cup milk
1   cup heavy cream
Dash of paprika

1. Fry onions and potatoes in oil over low flame until almost tender.
2. Add the pint of clam juice, salt, and pepper; cover and simmer for 10 minutes.
3. Add the 2 cans of minced clams with their juice (or fresh, cooked clams) and simmer another 15 minutes, covered.
4. Boil milk and cream together for one minute; then add to the chowder.
5. Sprinkle with paprika and serve piping hot.

This is another one of Bernice Hunt's recipes, true to her own style—simple and delicious.

bernice's pumpkin soup

1   large onion, sliced
1   tbsp. butter
1/2 tsp. curry powder
1½ tsp. salt
1   can unsweetened pumpkin (approximately 15 oz.)
4   cups chicken broth
1   large (16-oz.) carton yogurt (You'll have some left over for the topping.)
Nutmeg

1. Cook sliced onion in butter until transparent.
2. Add curry powder, salt, and pumpkin and blend until smooth.
3. Add chicken broth; bring to a boil, and remove from heat.
4. Add 1 cup of yogurt and blend well.
5. Serve in individual soup bowls topped with a dollop of yogurt and sprinkled with nutmeg.

My husband and I were invited for dinner one night by a Hungarian doctor we had recently met. He served us salad, soup, black bread, and wine. The food plus the exuberant conversation of his Hungarian guests made it a delightful evening. I loved the simplicity of the meal.

I have often scrambled to find the chili in order to remove it before serving. If it is left in too long, the soup can become too peppery. You just have to keep tasting and then hope you can find it.

The salad that accompanied this soup consisted of shredded cucumbers and green peppers in an oil and vinegar dressing with a generous dab of sour cream on top. Black bread and wine make it a true Hungarian meal, I'm told.

doctor frank's hungarian soup

1½ lb. Hungarian sweet sausage, cut into 2-inch pieces. (Kielbasa is the easiest to obtain but our Italian Pork Store makes something comparable which has no preservatives.)
1   large onion, sliced
2   tbsp. safflower oil
8   cups chicken broth
1/2 cup red or white wine
4   potatoes, peeled and quartered
Salt and pepper, to taste
1/4 to 1/2 head cabbage, shredded
1   red or green chili pepper
1   tbsp. paprika

1. Cut sausage into 2-inch pieces.
2. Brown sausage and onion in hot oil.
3. Place sausage in large pot with broth, wine, potatoes, salt and pepper.
4. Cook over medium heat until potatoes are done.
5. When potatoes are done, add cabbage, chili, pepper and paprika.
6. Simmer until cabbage is tender.

My husband's cousin, Cynthia, was mentioned earlier. Both of them were born on the same day only a year apart. They're both Scorpios with enormous amounts of energy. Maybe that is why Cynthia, who has a doctorate in sociology, can teach her college classes, write, lecture and then come home to cook an elaborate meal for twelve friends.

cynthia's cold green soup

3   medium zucchini, sliced
1   head broccoli
3   cups chicken stock
1   large (16-oz.) carton yogurt (1 cup for the soup, plus 1 tbsp. for each serving)
2   tbsp. curry powder
Salt and pepper, to taste

1. Chop broccoli, removing leaves and tough stems.

2. Cook zucchini and broccoli in 1 cup boiling water until tender.
3. Put the vegetables, along with their cooking water, in a blender.
4. Blend in chicken stock and 1 cup yogurt.
5. Add the 2 tbsp. curry powder, salt and pepper to taste.
6. Serve cold with 1 tbsp. yogurt in each bowl.

This is a very simple soup and is supposed to be very good for you. The recipe was given to me by Pauline Gomez who was experimenting with macrobiotic diets, trying to find good recipes that were also slimming. I understand that if you are willing to discard your usual breakfast rituals, it's a good way to start the day.

pauline's miso soup

2   cups carrots, diced
2   cups onions, diced
2   tbsp. safflower oil
8   cups water
6   tbsp. miso (Miso is a very nutritious soybean paste used for flavoring; it can be purchased at health food stores or oriental markets.)
2   green scallion tops, cut into 1-inch pieces

1. Saute carrots and onions in oil for 10 minutes.
2. Add water and simmer gently for half an hour.
3. Take out 1/4 cup of the hot broth and mix well with the miso.
4. Pour back into the soup and heat gently. (It is important not to boil the broth.)
5. Pour into individual bowls and garnish with scallion tops.

Everybody seems to have a recipe for cabbage soup. They're all a little different, and each person argues the merits of his own. I'm picking this one. It comes from a friend named Dassano who has red hair, mischievous eyes, and a lovely warm smile. Last summer she took her two small children and went to India to live on an ashram. Now she cooks nothing but vegetarian dishes, all of them good.

dassano's cabbage soup

1   tbsp. butter
2   onions, sliced
1   green pepper, sliced
1   medium cabbage, shredded
4   cups stock (meat, chicken or vegetable)
1   clove garlic
2   carrots, finely chopped
2   tbsp. honey
Juice from 1/2 lemon
1   14-oz. can tomato puree
Salt and pepper, to taste

1. Melt butter; add onions and green pepper; cook over low heat for ten minutes.
2. Add shredded cabbage and cook 5 minutes.
3. Add broth and all remaining ingredients; cook over low heat until vegetables are tender.

I don't know where this came from, but I suspect it was made by any one of a number of splendid Greek women who lived in my neighborhood when I was going to high school in Silver Spring, Maryland. It's easy and very good.

greek yogurt soup

2   large cucumbers, skinned and sliced
2   pints yogurt
1   clove garlic, pressed
3   tbsp. sesame oil
3   tbsp. lemon juice
1   tbsp. dill (or 1/4 cup fresh dill)

1. Put all ingredients, except dill, in a blender and blend well.
2. Chill and serve garnished with dill.

This has got to be the best gazpacho ever! It came from someone's elderly aunt in Massachusetts. I had it one evening in Greenwich Village, then never saw the people again. But Aunt Lucretia's soup will be with me forever.

aunt lucretia's gazpacho

1   medium onion, chopped
1   green pepper, seeded and chopped
1   cucumber, barely skinned and chopped
2   tomatoes, chopped
1½ tsp. Worcestershire sauce
1 or 2 drops Tabasco sauce
Juice from 1 clove garlic, pressed
1   quart tomato juice
2   hard boiled eggs
1/4 tsp. dry mustard
2   tbsp. olive oil
1   small green chili pepper, mashed
Juice from two lemons
1½ tbsp. wine vinegar
Salt and pepper, to taste
1   lemon or lime, sliced

1. Add chopped onion, green pepper, cucumber, tomatoes, Worcestershire sauce, tabasco sauce, garlic juice, lemon juice, wine vinegar to 1 quart tomato juice.
2. Chop egg whites into small pieces and add to mixture.
3. Mash egg yolks with the dry mustard and olive oil.
4. Add mashed chili pepper to egg mixture.
5. Add egg mixture to soup.
6. Stir well and chill.
7. Serve in individual bowls and garnish each with an ice cube and slice of lemon or lime.

My mother gave this recipe to me so long ago I'm sure she doesn't remember it. It's nice on a cold winter's evening with crusty French bread, red wine, fruit, and cheese.

mother's lentil soup

2   cups dried lentils
2   onions
6   cloves
Salt and pepper, to taste
2   tsp. chopped garlic
1   tbsp. olive oil (plus enough to fry croutons)
1   tsp. thyme
1   tbsp. wine vinegar
1   cup croutons, browned in olive oil

1. Wash lentils and soak overnight in 1 quart of water.
2. In the morning, add two more cups of water, 1 onion coarsely chopped, the other studded with the cloves, salt and pepper.
3. Let simmer until tender.
4. In a small pan, brown the garlic in 1 tbsp. olive oil.
5. Add garlic to lentils.
6. Discard cloves from the whole onion and chop.
7. Add the chopped onion to lentils along with thyme.
8. Bring to boil, stirring occasionally.
9. When soup reaches boil, add wine vinegar; reduce heat and simmer 5 minutes.
10. Serve with croutons fried in olive oil.

salads

salads

I think that salad must be my favorite category of food. For years I have followed one cardinal rule. For a tossed, green salad, the greens must be washed and dried thoroughly right before the meal. A salad spinner makes this an easy task. Just before serving the salad, the greens should be tossed with oil. To be sure each leaf is evenly coated, I toss twenty times before adding spices, vinegar, lemon juice, etc. If the greens have moisture on them, the oil will not adhere and the salad will be soggy. Although I sometimes make a prepared dressing, I really think this is the best way to make a tossed salad. I also like the ritual of eating salad after the main course with a good bread. One of the things I've learned from my friends is that you can be very imaginative about what you put into your salad, using unusual vegetables, fruits, seeds, and nuts. Although I usually prefer a green salad, there are many other wonderful varieties made with pastas, rice and vegetables. Remember, salad needn't always be relegated to a side dish. With a good bread and fruit, it can be a whole meal in itself.

Marcelle is a very nice French lady who used to cook for our friend Craig Braun. She finally returned to France, a loss to all of us. I can't imagine why I didn't write down every one of her recipes; they were that good.

marcelle's cucumbers

(Appetizer or Salad)

1 large cucumber
1 cup yogurt
3 cloves garlic, minced
Salt and pepper, to taste
2 tbsp. oil
1 tbsp. vinegar
2 tbsp. fresh parsley, chopped

1. Peel cucumber and chop into small cubes.
2. Mix yogurt, garlic, salt, and pepper.
3. Toss cucumbers with oil.
4. Add vinegar and stir.
5. Add yogurt mixture and mix thoroughly.
6. Arrange in individual bowls and sprinkle with parsley.

marcelle's avocado appetizer

(Appetizer or Salad)

3 tbsp. olive oil
2 tbsp. vinegar
1/2 tsp. dry mustard
Salt and pepper, to taste
3 ripe avocados
1/2 tsp. chives or parsley, chopped

1. Mix dressing of oil, vinegar, dry mustard, salt, and pepper.
2. Cut avocados lengthwise and remove pit.
3. Fill hollows with dressing and sprinkle with chives or parsley.

These are some of Jane Wilson's incredible combinations. You can readily see what I mean about imagination.

jane's summer salad

1   head leaf lettuce
1   head rugola
1   small zucchini, sliced
1   papaya or mango, skinned and sliced
1/2 cup peas, preferably fresh
4   tbsp. salad oil
2   tbsp. vinegar
Salt and pepper, to taste

1. Wash and dry lettuce and rugola and tear into bite-size pieces.
2. Add zucchini, fruit and peas to greens and toss in salad bowl with oil
3. Add vinegar, salt and pepper and toss again.

Note: Some people like a lot of vinegar, some just a little; test for your own preference.

jane's party salad

2   pre-cooked ham slices
6   apples
4   celery stalks
1   cup raisins
2   tbsp. curry powder
1   cup mayonnaise
Lettuce

1. Trim fat from ham and chop into small pieces.
2. Peel and core apples and chop into small pieces.
3. Chop celery.
4. Add raisins.
5. Mix curry powder and mayonnaise.
6. Add to salad and mix well.
7. Serve on bed of lettuce.

jane's macaroni salad

6   cups cooked macaroni
1   Bermuda onion, sliced
1   cup Cheddar or Muenster cheese, cubed
1   tbsp. savory
1/4 to 1/2 cup fresh dill, chopped
3 to 4 tbsp. olive oil
4   tbsp. vinegar
Salt and pepper, to taste

1. Combine all ingredients except oil, vingar, salt and pepper.
2. Add oil and toss thoroughly.
3. Add vinegar and toss again.
4. Add salt and pepper; taste for seasoning, and serve.

jane's rice salad

2   tbsp. butter
1   green pepper
2   cups rice
4   cups water
1   can (1-lb. 4-oz.) of pineapple chunks
1   cup soy nuts
1   tsp. dill weed
4   tbsp. safflower oil
3   tbsp. vinegar

1. Melt butter in frying pan.
2. Seed and chop green pepper.
3. Saute pepper and rice in butter until rice is golden.
4. Bring 4 cups water to boil and then add the rice, and green pepper to it and cook until rice is done.
5. When rice is cool, add the drained pineapple chunks and soy nuts and mix well.
6. Add the oil and dill and mix again.
7. Lastly, add the vinegar; mix, and serve.

This is another of Dorothy Friedman's unique combinations. It's best of course, with fresh peas, when you can get them.

dorothy's aduki salad

1   cup red aduki beans (found in health food stores)
3   cups water
1   medium onion, chopped
2   cups cooked peas
2   tbsp. oil
1   small red chili pepper, minced fine
3   tbsp. lemon juice
Salt and pepper, to taste

1. Soak aduki beans overnight in 3 cups of water.
2. Bring beans to boil; then simmer until just tender.
3. Drain aduki beans and combine with onion and peas.
4. Add oil and toss well.
5. Add chili pepper. (Tastes vary, so add this little by little, or it may be too hot.)
6. Add lemon juice, salt and pepper and mix well.

This is another of Pauline Gomez's macrobiotic recipes. Pauline met the lecturer and author, Michio Kushi, in Boston and found him to be a very good diagnostician as well as a dedicated advocate of a macrobiotic diet. It seems to me that this diet simply stresses a balanced way of eating and I am pleased that others are beginning to see its benefits, rather than viewing it as some hippie fad. It's worth investigating.

pauline's macrobiotic salad

1   bunch watercress, torn into small pieces
1   Bermuda onion, sliced
1   cup cooked chickpeas
2   tbsp. oil
2   tbsp. lemon juice
2   tbsp. Tahini (found in health food stores)
1   tbsp. Tamari (found in health food stores)

1. Mix watercress, sliced onion and chickpeas, and toss well with oil.
2. Add lemon juice and mix.
3. In a separate bowl, mix Tahini and Tamari.
4. Add to salad and mix well.

These are mine and they're all favorites.

greens and fruit

1   bunch watercress or romaine
2   oranges, skinned and sliced, or 1 small can of tangerines
1   small Bermuda onion, thinly sliced
4   tbsp. safflower oil
2   tbsp. lemon juice
Salt and pepper, to taste

1. Wash and dry watercress or romaine and tear into bite-sized pieces.
2. Arrange on individual salad plates.
3. Place orange slices (tangerines) and onions on top of greens.
4. Make a dressing of the oil, lemon juice, salt, and pepper.
5. Pour over salad and serve.

broccoli and tomato salad

1 head of broccoli
1 medium Bermuda onion, thinly sliced
3 tomatoes, sliced
4 tbsp. olive oil
Juice of 2 lemons
Salt and pepper, to taste

1. Cut broccoli into bite-sized pieces, including the most tender parts of the stalk.

2. Plunge into a large pot of boiling water and boil for 2 minutes.
3. Drain immediately.
4. Put broccoli, tomatoes, and onion into salad bowl.
5. Toss with olive oil.
6. Add lemon juice, salt, and pepper and mix well.

One year, my husband was asked to run marathon psychological groups for professionals in Argentina. Since the groups were long, he told everyone to contribute a dish to share for lunch. In the United States, this request was usually met with offerings of tunafish sandwiches, fruit, and potato chips. Not so in Argentina. This Argentine Eggplant was one of the dishes brought. (Potato Pie, listed in another section, was another.) Everything we ate in that country was always succulent!

argentine eggplant

1 large eggplant
3 tomatoes, chopped
2 onions, chopped
2 to 3 tbsp. olive oil
Juice of 3 lemons
Salt and pepper, to taste

1. Place eggplant in a large pan of boiling water and boil until done. (It should be tender, but not mushy.)
2. Peel the skin and drain the eggplant very well in a colander.
3. Chop into small pieces and place in bowl.
4. Add chopped tomatoes and onions to eggplant.
5. Toss with olive oil.
6. Add lemon juice, salt, and pepper and mix well.
7. Serve cold.

For a year, Marty and I, with our combined children, shared a house with Cindy and Cal and their combined children—our own experiment in communal living. A tremendous amount of cooking was involved as we often had as many as nine children sitting at our table. Cindy seemed well equipped to handle this. Having once been a nun, she had lived in a convent and was used to cooking for many people. Since then she has had a varied career, going from teacher, to massage instructor, while studying sky diving. Right now she works for the Y.M.C.A. preparing physical fitness programs for older people who have had heart attacks. As a sideline, she has embarked on something new, training as a marathon runner. This is her recipe, slightly modified, since I don't use commercial jellos.

cindy's jello salad

1   package Knox unflavored gelatin
1/2 cup cold water
1/2 cup raw sugar
1/2 tsp. salt
3   tbsp. vinegar
1/4 cup lime juice mixed with 1/2 cup water
1/2 cup mayonnaise
1/2 cup celery, chopped
1/2 cup green pepper, chopped
1/2 cup cottage cheese

1. Sprinkle gelatin over 1/2 cup cold water in a saucepan.
2. Stir over low heat for three minutes.
3. Remove from heat and add sugar, salt, vinegar, lime juice, and water; pour into jello mold and refrigerate.
4. Combine mayonnaise, celery, green pepper, and cottage cheese in a separate bowl.
5. When jello is slightly thickened, fold in cottage cheese mixture and chill until set.

The Midwest has its own particular style of cuisine and my ex-mother-in-law, a wonderful cook, had an approach to food that was typical there. Everything always tasted delicious and it was a treat to walk into her kitchen with roasts and deepdish cobblers baking and every burner on the stove cooking away. In later years, the food became too rich for me, but a few recipes have lingered on. Here's one.

christine's indiana coleslaw

1   medium cabbage, finely shredded
1   cup water
1/2 cup vinegar
1/4 cup sugar
Pinch of salt

1. Wash and shred cabbage.
2. Combine water, vinegar, sugar, and salt.
3. Pour over slaw and let stand at least one hour before serving.

I walked into a fancy delicatessen one day and saw this dish. It seemed so prohibitively expensive for such a tiny amount that I went right home, experimented a little, and made my own version.

chickpea salad

2   cups dried chickpeas (Canned chickpeas can be used, if you prefer, or are in a hurry, in which case they need no cooking.)
1   large onion, chopped
1   small green or red pepper, seeded and chopped
3   tbsp. parsley, chopped
Dash of red pepper or Tabasco Sauce
1/2 tsp. cumin
Salt and pepper, to taste
3   tbsp. olive oil
Juice of 2 lemons

1. Soak chickpeas overnight in 6 cups water, if dried ones are used.
2. Bring chickpeas to boil in the same water; reduce heat, and simmer until just tender.
3. Drain chickpeas.
4. To the chickpeas, add onion, pepper, 2 tbsp. of the chopped parsley, red pepper or Tabasco, cumin, salt and pepper.
5. Add olive oil and mix well.
6. Add lemon juice and stir.
7. Garnish with remaining tbsp. parsley.

I am including in this section two of my own dressings. The green mayonnaise is delicious with cold fish, avocados, and almost any raw vegetables. The mustard salad dressing will keep on the shelf and can be used for any salad with the exception of fruit.

green mayonnaise

2   cups mayonnaise
2   tbsp. scallions, finely chopped
4   tbsp. fresh parsley, finely chopped
4   tbsp. chives, finely chopped
4   tbsp. tarragaon, finely chopped
4   tbsp. watercress, finely chopped

1. Combine all ingredients.
2. Let stand for a while before using.

mustard salad dressing

2   tbsp. beer
2   tsp. dry mustard
1   cup olive oil
2   tbsp. dry white wine
2   tsp. dill
2   tsp. parsley
2   tsp. salt
Dash of pepper
1   clove garlic, crushed
1   medium onion, chopped fine

1. Mix beer and dry mustard.
2. Add remaining ingredients and stir.
3. Store in tightly closed glass jar and shake before using.

Many people say that soybeans are the healthiest and most inexpensive food available. However, I have found it hard to find recipes that I truly like. This one I discovered at a health food bar, and again I went home and tried to concoct one like it. It's probably my favorite soybean dish.

soybean salad

3 cups dried soybeans
2 quarts water
1 green pepper, seeded and chopped
2 medium onions, chopped
2 celery stalks, chopped
4 tbsp. pimento, chopped
4 small sweet pickles, diced
3 tsp. dill weed
Dash of Tabasco Sauce
Salt and pepper, to taste
2 cups mayonnaise

1. Soak soybeans overnight in the water.
2. Bring soybeans to a boil in the same water; reduce heat and simmer until done (usually 3 to 4 hours).
3. Add green pepper, onions, celery, pimento, and pickles to the drained soybeans, along with the dill weed, Tabasco, salt, and pepper.
4. Mix well.
5. Add mayonnaise and mix again. Since soybeans are rather bland, check the seasonings carefully. You may want less mayonnaise, more pickles or dill, etc.
   Experiment!

This is a recipe copied from a restaurant in New York that specializes in a combination of Chinese and health foods. I believe that it was also served as an appetizer.

marinated bean sprouts

1 lb. fresh bean sprouts
4 tbsp. green scallions, chopped
2 tbsp. red sweet pepper, finely chopped
2 tbsp. sesame oil
2 tbsp. tamari (soy sauce)
2 tbsp. wine vinegar

1. Rinse sprouts and drain.
2. Combine remaining ingredients and pour over sprouts.
3. Marinate overnight, or at least three hours.
4. Serve very cold.

My Greek friends again!

cold greek spinach salad

2   lbs. spinach (fresh)
2   tbsp. olive oil
2   tbsp. lemon juice
Salt and pepper, to taste
1   tbsp. sesame seeds

1. Wash the spinach and cook in a small amount of water.
2. Drain well in a colander and chop fine.
3. Toss with olive oil to coat spinach.
4. Add lemon juice, salt, pepper, and blend.
5. Sprinkle with sesame seeds and chill.

vegetables

vegetables

What can one say about vegetables? When you're a child, you usually hate them and, when you're an adult, you like them. If you don't eat much meat, you probably love them. These are all recipes that I like a lot and have even gotten children to eat without making awful faces.

Jeanne Humphries made this for one of our drumming and dancing sessions for which everyone brings a dish to share. She is a woman of many talents and interests, a fine musician and a teacher of children who also finds time to work on her doctorate in English.

jeanne's spicy cabbage

1 large onion, chopped
1 large green pepper, chopped
2 tbsp. oil
1/4 tsp. garlic powder
Salt and pepper, to taste
1 medium to large cabbage, shredded
1 tbsp. vinegar
1/4 tsp. cayenne pepper
4 tbsp. water
1 tsp. sugar

1. Saute onion and green pepper in oil until onions are golden.
2. Add garlic powder, salt, and pepper, and stir 1 minute more.
3. Add shredded cabbage and stir just enough to coat cabbage with the oil.
4. Add vinegar and cayenne pepper and cook for five minutes, stirring occasionally.
5. Sprinkle with water and sugar and cook 10 minutes more, or until tender.
6. Check for seasonings and serve hot or cold. (You may want to add more salt, cayenne pepper, vinegar, or sugar.)

My husband had a dish similar to this in a Manhattan restaurant. Taking a cue from me, he came home to try and reinvent it. It really helps to have fresh pea pods.

sesame peapods with garlic

2 to 3 large garlic cloves, minced
2 tbsp. olive oil
3/4 lb. fresh peapods or 2 boxes frozen (if you use frozen peapods, they must be very well drained.)
2 tbsp. soy sauce
1/4 cup sesame seeds

1. Brown garlic in 1 tbsp. of the olive oil.
2. Add the other tbsp. olive oil and peapods; stir fry 1 minute to coat peapods.
3. Add soy sauce and sesame seeds; mix well and serve.

I mentioned earlier that my friend Dorothy has a way with vegetables. These are all her dishes.

dorothy's turnips

1   large turnip or rutabaga
2   tbsp. butter
3   cloves garlic, minced
3   tbsp. soy sauce
3   tbsp. tahini (sesame seed paste)

1. Peel turnips and cut into small pieces.
2. Cook in two cups boiling water until done, but not mushy.
3. In a frying pan, melt butter and add minced garlic.
4. Saute garlic two minutes; then add soy sauce and tahini.
5. Stir mixture over low heat for another minute.
6. Add turnips, turn evenly to coat, and heat until turnips are warm.

dorothy's zucchini

4   cloves garlic, minced
2   tbsp. fresh, grated ginger
2   tbsp. oil
2   medium onions, sliced
4   cups zucchini, scrubbed and sliced
2   cups tomato sauce
2   tbsp. soy sauce
2   tbsp. fresh parsley, minced
1   tbsp. fresh basil, minced
Pepper, to taste

1. Saute garlic and ginger in oil for one minute.
2. Add onions and zucchini and cook 5 minutes.
3. Add tomato sauce, soy sauce, parsley, basil, and pepper and cook until done (20 to 30 minutes).

dorothy's zucchini and peas

1   clove garlic, minced
1   small onion, sliced
2   tbsp. cooking oil
3   zucchini, washed and sliced
1   box frozen peas (unless you can get 2
    cups of fresh ones)
2   tsp. fresh basil, minced
2   tsp. fresh tarragon, minced
Salt and pepper, to taste

1. Fry garlic and onions in oil for a few minutes.
2. Add zucchini, peas, basil, tarragon, salt and pepper, and saute gently until done, approximately 20 minutes.
3. Stir vegetables occasionally to keep from sticking.

dorothy's cabbage

2/3 stick butter
1   tbsp. oil
2   tsp. mustard seeds
2   tsp. cumin
2   tsp. tumeric
1   tsp. freshly grated ginger
3   cloves garlic, minced
1/2 large cabbage, shredded
4   medium onions, chopped
1   green pepper, seeded and chopped
Salt and pepper, to taste

1. Melt 2/3 stick butter with 1 tbsp. oil.
2   Add mustard seeds, cumin, tumeric, ginger, and garlic and cook for two minutes over low heat while stirring.
3. Add vegetables to seasonings and saute until cabbage is done, stirring occasionally.

These are Pauline's again. She is very weight-conscious and you can be sure that all of her recipes are slimming.

pauline's wok broccoli

1   head of broccoli
2   tbsp. safflower oil
1   clove garlic, peeled and sliced
2   tbsp. soy sauce
2   tbsp. chicken broth

1. Wash broccoli and separate into small flowerets.
2. Parboil by placing broccoli in pot of boiling water for two minutes.
3. Drain immediately. (Save water for soups.)
4. Heat oil in wok and brown garlic.
5. Add broccoli and stir fry for a couple of minutes over high heat. (To stir fry, simply flip over the ingredients again and again as you're cooking. You can use Chinese utensils. I usually use wooden spoons.)
6. Turn heat to low, add soy sauce and chicken broth and cover.
7. Cook for three minutes and serve.

pauline's souffle

2   lbs. fresh spinach
1   large clove garlic, chopped
1   medium onion, chopped
2   tbsp. olive oil
3   eggs, beaten
1   cup ricotta cheese
Salt and pepper, to taste
1   small (8-oz.) mozzarella cheese

1. Wash and drain spinach.
2. Saute garlic and onion in olive oil for 3 minutes.
3. Add well-drained spinach; reduce heat, cover and cook until spinach is tender.
4. Chop the spinach and drain the spinach-onion mixture in a colander.
5. Butter a baking dish.
6. Mix ricotta cheese with eggs and pour into baking dish.
7. Add drained spinach, salt, and pepper and mix well.
8. Slice mozzarella and spread over casserole.
9. Bake, uncovered, in 350-degree oven for one half hour.

This one takes more time but it is one of my favorites and I serve it as a main course in place of fish or poultry.

pauline's spinach lasagna

PART ONE
Tomato Sauce

1/2 large onion, chopped
1   small green pepper, chopped
2   cloves garlic, chopped
2   tbsp. olive oil
1   large can Italian plum tomatoes (approximately 1 lb.)
1/4 cup red wine
1   bay leaf

2   tbsp. parsley
1   tsp. basil
1   tsp. oregano

1. Saute onions, green pepper, and garlic in olive oil.
2. Add remaining ingredients and simmer for one half hour.

PART TWO
Cheese-Spinach Filling

1   large onion, chopped
2   cloves garlic, chopped
2   tbsp. olive oil
2   lbs. ricotta cheese
1/2 lb. Parmesan cheese, grated
1/2 lb. spinach, washed and chopped

3   eggs, beaten
2   tbsp. parsley
Salt and pepper, to taste

1. Saute onion and garlic in olive oil.
2. Add remaining ingredients; mix well.

PART THREE
The Casserole

1   tbsp. oil
1/2 lb. lasagna noodles

1. Bring 4 quarts of water to a rapid boil; add oil and then add noodles one by one, slowly to prevent sticking. Boil for 10 minutes.
2. Drain noodles well.

3. Butter a flat baking dish.
4. Alternate layers of noodles, cheese-spinach mixture, and tomato sauce, making sure to end up with the tomato sauce.
5. Cover with foil and bake at 350 degrees for 40 minutes.
6. Remove foil and bake 10 minutes more.
7. Cut into squares and serve.

These are Jane Wilson's again and each has her unique touch. The puree is a really memorable dish, like nothing I have ever tasted before.

jane's summer vegetable medley - no. 1

1/2 lb. asparagus, preferably fresh
3   tbsp. oil
1/2 cup raisins
2   medium zucchini, cut into small pieces
2   yellow squash, cut into small pieces

1. Cut asparagus into 2-inch pieces, discarding tough ends.
2. Heat oil in wok.
3. Stir fry all ingredients until done. (This shouldn't take longer than 5 minutes and the vegetables should still be slightly crunchy.)

jane's summer vegetable medley - no. 2

1   medium eggplant
1   plantain or 2 bananas
3   tomatoes
3   tbsp. oil

1. Cut eggplant into small pieces, leaving skin on.
2. Peel plantains or bananas, then cut first lengthwise, then in halves.
3. Cut tomatoes in quarters or eighths.
4. Heat oil in wok.
5. Add eggplant and stir fry until almost done.
6. Add plantain or bananas and stir fry 2 minutes more.
7. Add tomatoes; stir fry 1 or 2 minutes and serve.

jane's wok squash

3   tbsp. oil
2   yellow squash, cut into small pieces
2   green zucchini, cut into small pieces
2   tart apples, peeled and cut into small pieces
4   tbsp. sesame seeds

1. Heat oil in wok.
2. Add yellow squash and zucchini and stir fry until done. (Do not overcook.)
3. Add apples and stir fry 1 or 2 minutes more.
4. Sprinkle with sesame seeds and serve.

jane's orange puree

6   carrots, peeled and sliced
6   parsnips, peeled and sliced
1/4 to 1/2 cup heavy cream
Salt and pepper, to taste

1.   Boil carrots and parsnips separately in salted water until tender. (Save cooking waters for soups.)
2.   Put in blender with cream and puree. (The amount of cream used depends on the consistency you prefer.)
3.   Add salt and pepper to taste.
4.   Serve warm.

Frances Miller is a wonder! She's an artist, a writer, a woman whose zest for living has carried her well into a vintage year. She is the ideal role model for me and many others who wonder how we'll enjoy our later years. An environmentalist, a vegetarian, she is creative and courageous. Right now she is publishing the second part of her autobiography, with one more installment to come, and she has just recently exhibited her paintings at a Hamptons gallery.

frances's soybeans

1   large green pepper
3   cups cooked soybeans
1   clove pressed garlic
1   tsp. chili powder
2 to 3 tbsp. soy sauce
Salt and pepper, to taste

1.   To cook soybeans, soak overnight in 4 quarts water. Bring to a boil and boil 5 minutes. Reduce heat and cook until ten-der (3-4 hours). Drain, leaving 1 cup liquid.
2.   Slice green pepper into thin strips.
3.   Cook pepper in 1/4 cup boiling water for 3 minutes.
4.   Heat soybeans and add garlic, chili powder, soy sauce, salt, and pepper. (Taste as you go; you may want to add more of something.)
5.   Top with drained pepper strips and serve.

frances miller's vegetaria

3   carrots
1/4 head cabbage
1   green pepper
2   yellow squash
2   fresh tomatoes
2   onions
1   small eggplant
1/3 cup soy sauce
4   tbsp. honey
1   bouillon cube dissolved in 2 tbsp.
    water
1   tbsp. parsley
1   tsp. basil
Salt and pepper, to taste
1   cup raisins
1/4 cup grated Romano cheese

1. Wash and cut all vegetables, peeling when necessary.
2. Mix soy sauce, honey, the bouillon cube dissolved in water, and seasonings.
3. In a covered pot, over low heat, cook vegetables and raisins in the soy mixture, adding more water if necessary.
4. When vegetables are done, sprinkle with grated Romano cheese.

This is another one from my former mother-in-law. It is delicious made with the kind of beans and tomatoes you find in Indiana.

christine's indiana green beans

2   lbs. fresh green beans
1   piece of ham or ham hock for flavoring
2   nice ripe red tomatoes, chopped (beef-steak size)
2   sweet onions, chopped
Salt and pepper, to taste

1. In a covered pot, cook green beans and ham in 4 cups water until tender. The beans should stew slowly (about 2 hours) to absorb the meat flavor, a very different method from short cooking.)
2. Drain beans; add salt and pepper to taste.
3. Serve beans with plenty of tomatoes and onions sprinkled on top.

One evening a new guest appeared at one of our communal meals. He has proved a very welcome addition. Don Kennedy is a local artist, a sculptor, a musician and an avid gardener. A man of many interests, his great passion at this moment is building a huge piece of sculpture, the biggest he has ever attempted. He was immediately singled out for praise that evening because of his delectable contribution. This is it.

don's zucchini tempura

4 or 5 medium zucchini, grated
1   medium onion, grated
2   cloves garlic, thinly sliced
Rosemary, basil, or chives (optional)
2   eggs
1/4 cup milk
1/2 cup wheat or rice flour
Safflower oil

1. Mix zucchini, onion, and garlic in a bowl. (You may add any of the spices at this time; fresh is always preferable.)
2. Beat the two eggs and add milk.
3. Sift the flour into this mixture and blend to the consistency of pancake batter.

4. Add grated vegetables to batter and mix slightly.
5. In a good-sized frying pan, pour 1/2 inch safflower oil and heat it for 4 or 5 minutes.
6. With a small spoon, place dollops of the squash mixture in the hot oil, making sure that they are not larger than 2 inches across and that they do not touch.
7. Brown on both sides, then drain on a paper towel. (Cooking should take about 4 or 5 minutes; you can test by breaking one apart.)
8. Serve the tempura either hot or cold.
9. You can make a simple dipping sauce for the tempura by mixing tamari sauce with some chopped chives.

Bessie Ahouris was one of our closest Greek friends when I lived in Silver Spring as a teenager. She is a warm friendly woman who raised four daughters, helped raise numerous grandchildren, and often summoned us to her house to sample Greek pastries and other dishes as well. This is one of the other dishes, convenient and easy to prepare ahead of time.

bessie's greek lima beans

1   lb. dried lima beans
2   medium onions, chopped
2   cloves garlic, chopped
2   tsp. oregano
1   bay leaf
Salt and pepper, to taste
1   large can tomatoes (about 2 lbs.)
1½ cups bread crumbs

1. Soak lima beans overnight in 2 quarts water.
2. Cook lima beans in water with onions, garlic, oregano, bay leaf, salt and pepper until tender (about 2 hours).
3. Drain beans and put in a casserole with the canned tomatoes, mixing well.
4. Top with bread crumbs and bake in a 350-degree oven for 1/2 hour.

My mother-in-law, Marcia, is a very attractive woman, with a good sense of humor. She is also a consummate shopper, getting great value for her money. (She should probably give classes in "how-to-shop.") This dish is hers; it was absolutely foreign to me and I loved it.

marcia's turnips

1   large turnip
1   medium onion, chopped
Mayonnaise
Salt and pepper, to taste

1. Peel the raw turnip and grate it as you would grate cabbage for slaw.
2. Add enough mayonnaise to make a creamy slaw. The amount will depend on the size of the turnip.
3. Add the chopped onion, salt and pepper to taste and mix well.

The rest of the recipes in this section are mine, gathered over the years and trifled with.

oriental citrus squash

3 small acorn squash
1 cup orange marmalade
1 tbsp. minced ginger
1 tbsp. lemon juice
2 tbsp. butter
Sprinkling of nutmeg

1. Cut squash in halves and remove seeds.
2. Place squash cut-side down in a shallow baking dish with just enough water to lightly cover bottom of dish; bake at 350 degrees for 45 minutes.
3. Mix marmalade with ginger and lemon juice.
4. Turn squash over and brush with butter, then fill cavities with the marmalade mixture.
5. Sprinkle with nutmeg and bake 15 minutes more, adding water to bottom of pan if necessary.

beets and tops

2 bunches of beets with nice fresh tops
1 small onion, chopped fine
1 tbsp. olive oil
Salt and pepper, to taste
2 tbsp. lemon juice

1. Cut off beet tops and cook beets in boiling water until tender.
2. Remove beet skins and slice.
3. Wash beet tops extremely well and drain; cut into small pieces.
4. Saute onion and beet tops in olive oil until tender.
5. Add salt, pepper, and lemon juice.
6. Serve warm beets with the tops. (Tops may also be served warm or chilled in a separate dish.)

eggplant parmesan

1   medium eggplant
2   eggs, beaten
2   cups breadcrumbs
3/4 cup oil
1   can tomato puree (16 oz.)
1   cup red wine
Salt and pepper, to taste
1   small carton ricotta cheese (16 oz.)
1   small package mozzarella cheese (8 oz.),
    sliced
1/2 cup freshly grated Parmesan cheese

1. Wash eggplant and cut it, unpeeled, into thin slices.
2. Arrange 2 beaten eggs in one pan and the bread crumbs in another.
3. Dip eggplant slices first in the egg and then in the bread crumbs to coat.
4. Heat some of the oil in a large frying pan over medium heat.
5. Shake off loose crumbs and brown eggplant in oil, adding more oil when needed. The eggplant will soak up a lot of oil. Turn once to brown other side.
6. Drain eggplant slices on paper towel.
7. Combine tomato puree, wine, salt and pepper.
8. Arrange a layer of eggplant in a shallow baking dish.
9. Pour part of sauce over eggplant; then add some of the ricotta cheese.
10. Continue layering like this with eggplant, sauce, and ricotta, until all eggplant has been used.
11. Top with sliced mozzarella and sprinkle with Parmesan cheese.
12. Cover with foil and bake in a 350-degree oven for 1/2 hour.
13. Remove foil and continue baking for another 15 minutes.

string beans and yogurt

1   lb. fresh string beans
1   cup yogurt
1/2 cup chopped onion
1   tbsp. honey
Salt and pepper, to taste
1   cup grated Parmesan cheese
1/2 cup sesame seeds

1. Steam string beans until just tender.
2. Blend yogurt, honey, chopped onion, salt, and pepper.
3. Put beans in lightly oiled casserole.
4. Pour yogurt sauce over beans and mix.
5. Sprinkle with grated cheese, then with sesame seeds.
6. Cover and bake in a 350-degree oven for 1/2 hour.
7. Uncover and bake 10 minutes more.

This is delicious—simple and nutritious. All you have to do is cultivate a taste for tofu.

simple baked tofu

Tofu—enough to cut into 12 bite-sized
    squares
1   clove garlic, minced
2   scallions, cut into 1-inch pieces
1/3 cup soy sauce

1. Put the bite-sized pieces of tofu in a small baking dish.
2. Add garlic, scallions, and soy sauce. (Reserve a few pieces of scallion for garnish.)
3. Bake in a 350-degree oven for 20 minutes.
4. Before serving, add a few pieces of fresh scallion on top.
    Note: Equally good, and good for you, is the same recipe with a substitution. Instead of soy sauce, use 2 tsp. miso mixed with enough water to make 1/3 cup.

summer string beans

1   lb. string beans
1   clove garlic, minced
1   medium onion, chopped
1   large tomato, chopped
1   small green pepper, seeded and
     chopped
2   tbsp. fresh parsley
Cooking oil
Salt and pepper, to taste

1. Steam string beans until just tender.
2. Saute garlic and onions in 2 tbsp. oil.
3. Add tomatoes and green pepper to onions; cover, and simmer 10 minutes.
4. Pour over warm beans; add salt and pepper, sprinkle with parsley and serve.

pasta

pasta

I love pasta. Doesn't everyone? I have a special memory of myself and a friend sitting across from the Vatican in Rome one early afternoon. We had very little money and, for lunch, we chose an inexpensive sidewalk cafe. I have always considered the meal we had there one of my most memorable feasts, though we ate only pasta with butter, grated parmesan cheese, and freshly ground black pepper, washing it down with a glass of red table wine. Such are the pleasures of life!

I'm sure most people know how to prepare the standard spaghetti with meat balls or meat sauce. I think these are even better.

These first recipes were given to me by my friend and gourmet cook, Vincenzo de Persiis. Artist, architect, caring gardener, and witty conversationalist, he is a man whose artistic touch is evident throughout his house, and especially in his kitchen.

vincenzo's anchovy spaghetti

1 stick butter (¼-lb.)
2 cans flat anchovies in olive oil (2 oz. each)
8 cloves garlic, sliced
6 tbsp. olive oil
Freshly ground pepper, to taste
1 lb. spaghetti
1 cup grated Parmesan cheese

1. Melt butter over low heat and add anchovies, including the oil.
2. Mash anchovies slowly, until all the pieces are dissolved in the butter.
3. Meanwhile in a separate pan, brown garlic slices lightly in olive oil.
4. Cook spaghetti in a large pot of boiling water.
5. Drain pasta; pour both the anchovy and the garlic sauce over spaghetti.
6. Sprinkle with freshly ground black pepper.
7. Serve with grated Parmesan cheese.

vincenzo's tuna spaghetti

2 cloves garlic, minced
1 cup fresh parsley, minced (or 4 tbsp. dried parsley)
6 tbsp. olive oil
1 large (10-oz.) can chunk light tuna, drained
1 tsp. oregano
1/2 cup dry white wine
Hot chili (optional)
1 large can (about 2 lbs.) Italian tomatoes
Grated Parmesan or Romano cheese

1. Saute garlic and parsley in olive oil until garlic is golden.
2. Add tuna and cook, chopping with a fork until chunks have disintegrated.
3. Add oregano and wine (a piece of hot chili may be added with the wine, if you like a spicy sauce); cook until most of the wine has evaporated. (This takes only a few moments.)
4. Add the can of Italian tomatoes without the juice, and mash tomatoes thoroughly.
5. Simmer, covered, 10 minutes.
6. Cook 1 lb. spaghetti, drain, and serve with the tuna sauce on top and a side dish of grated Parmesan or Romano cheese.

The Pesto Sauce can be prepared beforehand and stored in a covered container with a slight film of olive oil on top to prevent darkening. You can also make a large batch to store in the freezer. If you freeze it, omit Step 2. Thaw the sauce overnight; then follow Step 2 and proceed.

vincenzo's linguine al pesto

1¼ cups fresh basil
1/2 cup pine nuts
2   cloves garlic, minced
1   cup olive oil
1½ cups grated Parmesan cheese
Salt and pepper, to taste
1   lb. spaghetti

1. Place 1¼ cups fresh basil, 1/2 cup pine nuts, garlic, and 1/2 cup of the olive oil in a blender and blend until smooth.
2. Add the other 1/2 cup of olive oil, 1/2 cup of the Parmesan cheese, salt, and pepper and blend again. This is the Pesto Sauce.
3. Cook 1 lb. spaghetti, drain and pour pesto over top.
4. Mix well at the table and serve with the remaining grated cheese.

The secret of this dish is to add the right amount of herbs and garlic and to serve it hot.

my green spaghetti

1/4 cup olive oil
4   cloves garlic, minced
2   tsp. basil
3   tbsp. oregano
4   tbsp. parsley, minced
1   lb. spaghetti
3   tsp. butter
Salt and pepper, to taste
1   cup grated Parmesan cheese

1. In a small frying pan, heat olive oil.
2. Brown garlic in oil.
3. Add basil, oregano, parsley, salt, and pepper; saute 1 minute more.
4. Cook spaghetti in a large pot of boiling water.
5. Drain and toss with the butter.
6. Add olive oil with herbs and toss well.
7. Check seasonings; adding more if necessary.
8. Add Parmesan cheese, toss again and serve.

This comes from another Italian friend, a painter and sculptor by the name of Franco Ciarlo. Franco is a witty and stimulating conversationalist now living in New York, who, like Vincenzo, has a great flair for the dramatic. He gives it full play when he adds the finishing touches to this dish.

franco's pasta
with sausage and brandy

4 sweet Italian sausages (or 1 per person)
1 pint heavy cream
1 large onion, chopped
2 tbsp. olive oil
1 large can Italian tomatoes with basil (about 2 lbs.), salt and pepper to taste (best when heavily peppered)
4 shot glasses of inexpensive brandy
1 cup grated Parmesan cheese
1 lb. rigatoni (noodles)

1. Remove casing from sausage.
2. Brown sausage meat in frying pan; you may not need to add any oil (there is a lot of fat in most sausages).
3. When sausage is brown, add the cream and simmer over low heat until thick, stirring frequently. (This should take about 30 minutes.)
4. In another pan, saute onion in olive oil until golden.
5. Add the tomatoes, salt, and pepper and cook 1/2 hour.
6. Combine sauces in a large frying pan.
7. In the meantime, add the rigatoni to a large pot of boiling water, and cook al dente (not too soft); drain.
8. Put the rigatoni in a large serving dish, add sauce, and mix.
9. Heat brandy and ignite.
10. Pour flaming brandy over pasta.
11. Serve with Parmesan cheese.

Armand LaMacchia teaches in elementary school, is a fine drummer who plays with a country music group on weekends, and seems to have progressed from a good cook to a superb one over the years.

armand's marinara sauce

6-8 fresh tomatoes (If fresh tomatoes are unavailable, substitute 1 2-lb. can of whole tomatoes, making sure they are well drained.)
6   cloves garlic, minced
4   cups fresh parsley, minced
1/4 to 1/2 cup olive oil
Salt and pepper, to taste
1/4 cup Romano cheese (plus extra for sprinkling)

1. Immerse tomatoes in boiling water for 2 minutes, then peel.
2. Cut out core and any green spots and let tomatoes drain.
3. Saute garlic and parsley in olive oil for about 4 minutes. (Don't allow garlic to turn brown.)
4. Add tomatoes and chop slightly with spoon.
5. Add salt and pepper to taste.
6. Add grated Romano cheese and simmer sauce 20 to 30 minutes.
7. Serve over pasta with extra cheese.

If I had chosen myself, I couldn't have found a better sister-in-law than the one my brother picked for me. Linda is pretty, perky, and just plain fun to be with. She *has* to possess an easy-going disposition since she takes a lot of good-natured teasing from my incorrigible younger brother Jeffrey, of whom I'm also very fond. One night, despite the ribbing she was getting about her tennis game, Linda managed to put this dish together for our supper. I like it because it's surprisingly light, good for a meatless dinner, and can be prepared in advance.

linda's stuffed shells

1   medium onion, diced
1   tbsp. olive oil
1   28-oz. can tomatoes
1   6-oz. can tomato paste
2   tsp. brown sugar
1   tsp. oregano
1½ tsp. salt
1/4 tsp. pepper
1   12-oz, package jumbo macaroni shells
1   package creamed spinach
1   15-oz. carton ricotta cheese
1   tsp. salt
1/4 tsp. pepper
1   8-oz. package mozzarella cheese

1. To prepare tomato sauce, saute onion in oil in a heavy sauce pan.
2. Add the tomatoes, tomato paste, sugar, oregano, 1½ tsp. salt, and 1/4 tsp. pepper.
3. Stir over high heat and break up the tomatoes with a wooden spoon.
4. When mixture comes to a boil, reduce heat, cover and simmer 20 minutes.
5. Meanwhile, boil a large pot of water and cook shells as directed.
6. Prepare the creamed spinach as directed. (You can make your own creamed spinach from scratch, of course.)
7. Pour the cooked spinach into a bowl and add the ricotta cheese, 1 tsp. salt and 1/4 tsp. pepper; stir.
8. Shred the mozzarella cheese, add to spinach and stir again.
9. Pre-heat oven to 350 degrees.
10. Drain the shells and fill each shell with about 1 tbsp. of the spinach mixture.
11. Cover the bottom of a flat lasagna-type pan with some of the tomato sauce.
12. Arrange the shells in pan over sauce.
13. Top with remaining tomato sauce.
14. Cover with foil and bake 30 minutes.

potatoes, rice,
corn meal

potatoes, rice, corn meal

This is a small selection of filling dishes which are not too expensive to make, can be served as side dishes or with salads and, in the right combinations, can be the basis of a whole meal.

This is the other Argentinian dish mentioned earlier. It can be served either hot or cold, taken on picnics—eaten any time of the day or night, for that matter. I have seen some of my friends in Argentina flip it up and over. I have not been able to master that feat, so have my own improvisation.

argentine potato pie

2   large onions, chopped (enough for one cup)
1   green pepper, seeded and diced
6   large potatoes, peeled and sliced thin
1/2 cup safflower oil
6   eggs
Salt and pepper, to taste

1. Fry onions, green pepper, and potatoes in oil over low to medium heat until potatoes are tender. This will take 20 to 30 minutes. The potatoes should be turned frequently to prevent sticking and you may have to add more oil.

2. Beat eggs and pour over potatoes.

3. Add salt and pepper and cover, cooking slowly until the egg sets. You will probably have to tilt the pan every so often and let the egg run out to the sides of the pan to cook. This is easier than trying to flip it over.

4. Cut in pie-shaped wedges and serve hot or cold.

Here is another Hoosier dish. My oldest son, Aaron, requested it so often that he would finally bribe me to make it by volunteering to peel and cut all the potatoes. I can still see him meticulously cutting them to identical sizes and shapes, all with the greatest precision. Eventually, he took over the complete preparation himself, and I consider it his dish.

aaron's potatoes au gratin

6 to 8 large potatoes, peeled and cubed
1   lb. cheese (cheddar, Wisconsin, store cheese, etc.) diced
2   tbsp. flour
Salt and pepper, to taste
2   cups milk

1. Arrange half the potatoes in a Pyrex loaf baking dish or something similar.
2. Cover with half of the diced cheese.
3. Sprinkle with 1 tbsp. of the flour and add some of the salt and pepper.
4. Add remaining potatoes, then the rest of the cheese.
5. Add the second tbsp. flour, and more salt and pepper.
6. Pour milk over the casserole and cover with foil.
7. Bake at 400 degrees for 1/2 hour.
8. Remove foil and bake 20 minutes more.
9. Prick potatoes with fork to make sure they're done.

I once went to a "bring-your-own-dish" supper and had a lovely, cold, rice dish. It had been made by an Indian lady who was not present, so I had to go home and try to approximate it. The spices, vinegar, and oil may vary in quantity; it depends on one's palate.

indian rice

1   medium onion, chopped
1   cup raisins
2   tbsp. butter
4   cups cooked white rice
5   tbsp. oil (I used safflower oil)
Seeds of 8 cardamom pods
1   tbsp. tumeric
1   tbsp. cinnamon
1   tsp. nutmeg
1   cup pine nuts
2   tbsp. honey
4   tbsp. vinegar

1. Saute onions and raisins in butter until onions are golden.
2. Add onions and raisins to cooked rice and mix well.
3. Add the 5 tbsp. oil to rice and mix thoroughly.
4. Add all spices, pine nuts and the honey and stir again.
5. Add vinegar, mix, and chill before serving.

The following are my own experiments. The rice dish is a particular favorite. I believe it is not only good for you but a big pot of it can carry you through a whole week. If you can't find wheat berries start with the brown rice. It's good that way too. This first dish is not as complicated as it looks, nor does it take too long. Basically, it is just cooked rice mixed with vegetables (or any leftovers) and a little soy sauce.

brown rice and wheat berries

1/2 cup wheat berries (These can be purchased in most health food stores.)
1½ cups brown rice
1   large onion, chopped
2   cloves garlic, chopped
5   tbsp. oil
1   small carrot, chopped
1/2 small green pepper, chopped
1   stalk celery, chopped
1/4 cup soy sauce
2   scallion tops, chopped for garnish

1. Bring 1 cup water to a boil.
2. Add the wheat berries and bring to boil again.
3. Lower heat, cover, and cook 20 minutes.
4. Add 3 more cups of water to wheat berries and bring to boil again.
5. Add brown rice, cover, lower heat and cook until rice is done (approximately 45 minutes).
6. In a large frying pan, saute onions and garlic in 2 tbsp. of the oil for 2 minutes.
7. Add carrots, green pepper, and celery and saute for 5 minutes more.
8. Drain rice well and add to vegetables in the frying pan along with the other 3 tbsp. oil.
9. Cook over low heat for five minutes, stirring occasionally.
10. Add soy sauce, mix well, and cook a few minutes more.
11. Garnish with the scallion tops.

my corn meal dinner

6   cups water
2   cups corn meal (not degerminated)
1/2 tsp. salt
1/4 cup butter
1/2 cup grated Parmesan cheese (plus more
     for sprinkling)
2   onions, chopped
2   green peppers, chopped
2   tomatoes, chopped
2   tbsp. oil
4   cups tomato sauce or puree
1   tsp. basil
1   tsp. oregano
1/4 tsp. garlic salt
Salt and pepper, to taste

1. Bring 6 cups water to a boil.
2. Pour corn meal in slowly, stirring constantly (but it will get lumpy, no matter what anyone says).
3. Add 1/2 tsp. salt and the butter and cook over low heat for 20 minutes, stirring frequently.
4. Add Parmesan cheese and cook 5 minutes more.
5. Pour into a buttered Pyrex dish.
6. Saute onions and green peppers in oil until onions are transparent.
7. Add tomatoes and cook 5 minutes.
8. Add tomato sauce or puree, herbs, garlic salt, salt and pepper; cook 10 minutes.
9. Pour sauce over corn meal and bake in a 400-degree oven for 15 minutes.
10. Sprinkle with more Parmesan cheese when serving, if desired.

fish

fish

Only the freshest!!! We live in an area where fresh fish is always available, although in the winter there is not as much variety as in the other seasons. Only after living here have I begun to realize that much of the fish that I have eaten before was not terribly fresh, and I cringe to think that there was a time when frozen commercial fish was in my freezer. Fish should never taste or smell fishy—even when raw! So, to make this introduction short and to the point, find a good fish market and take advantage of its freshest catch.

This is the first dish that I learned to make when I got out of my frozen fish stage. I don't remember where I found it.

cuban fish with almonds

2   onions, 1 chopped, 1 sliced
2   cloves garlic, chopped
2   tbsp. olive oil
1   cup slivered almonds
3   tbsp. fresh parsley, chopped fine
3   tbsp. beef broth
3   tbsp. butter
1/2 tsp. thyme
6   fish fillets (2-3 lbs., preferably skinned, and thinly sliced, flounder, weakfish, etc.)
3   tbsp. lemon juice
Salt and pepper, to taste

1. Saute chopped onion and garlic in olive oil for 5 minutes.
2. Add almonds and parsley and cook another 5 minutes, stirring frequently.
3. Reduce heat to low; add broth, and cook 5 minutes more.
4. Melt butter in a large ovenproof casserole.
5. Add onion slices and sprinkle with thyme.
6. Put fillets in dish, making sure that they don't overlap.
7. Sprinkle with lemon juice, salt, and pepper.
8. Bake in 350-degree oven for 15 minutes.
9. Pour parsley and almond sauce over fish and bake 20 minutes more, or until done.

jane wilson's hibachi clams

4   tbsp. butter
2   cloves garlic, minced
1/2 tsp. thyme, fresh if available
2   dozen clams

1. Melt butter and saute garlic for 2 minutes.
2. Add thyme and cook 1 minute more.
3. Open clams and place on hot hibachi (or put under broiler).
4. Spoon sauce over clams and cook until done (6 to 8 minutes).

When my husband and I visited the island of St. John's in the Caribbean, we found a small, unpretentious restaurant called Rick's. Rick had a very simple menu and it consisted of the fish that he had caught that day. We would drive by and see him outside cleaning the fish. He'd wave and smile and then we'd drive back at night to sample it. He willingly gave me this recipe. Lots of lime juice and hot pepper give it its marvelous flavor.

rick's fish

6   fish fillets (about 3 to 4 lbs. of floun-
    der, weakfish, sole, etc.)
Juice from four limes
1   egg, beaten
1   cup bread crumbs (more if needed)
Cayenne pepper
Salt and pepper, to taste
6   tbsp. safflower oil

1. Dip fillets in lime juice and let them marinate 15 to 30 minutes.
2. Dip fillets in the beaten egg.
3. Mix bread crumbs, lots of cayenne pepper, and the salt and pepper. (The amount of cayenne that you use depends on how spicy you like your food. Start with 1/4 tsp. and experiment.)
4. Dip fillets in bread crumb mixture, coating well.
5. Heat oil in frying pan and fry fillets over high heat, turning once; when fish flakes easily, it is done.

This is simple, but good, and it comes from Pauline Gomez again.

pauline's mussels in beer

4   dozen mussels
1   bottle beer
1   cup parsley, chopped

1. Scrub mussels thoroughly under cold water.
2. Pour beer into large pot and bring to boil.
3. Add mussels and parsley, cover, and steam until done, shaking pan once or twice. (Usually, this takes about 5 or 6 minutes.)

This mussel dish comes from Dorothy Friedman. It's a little more work, but definitely worth it.

dorothy's mussels in garlic sauce

2   cloves garlic, minced
2   scallions, chopped
1   cup fresh parsley, chopped
2   tbsp. butter
1¼ cups white wine
4   dozen mussels, washed and scrubbed

1. Saute garlic, scallions, and parsley in butter for a few minutes.
2   Add wine and simmer slowly for 10 to 15 minutes.
3. Transfer to a large pot and bring to boil.
4. Add mussels, cover, and steam until mussels open (usually 5 to 6 minutes).

These two recipes come from a beautiful Japanese woman named Rako who lived in my building when I first moved to New York. She has four handsome sons, hair down to her waist, and a charming giggle. Over the years, we have lost track of each other, but I still make her recipes and am reminded of her, a way of keeping in touch perhaps.

fish rako

1/2 cup soy sauce
1   tsp. raw sugar
1/4 cup peanut oil
1   large clove of garlic, minced
2   tsp. fresh ginger, grated
2   lbs. fish fillets (flounder, weakfish, blue-fish, etc.)
1/4 cup sesame seeds.

1. Combine all ingredients except fish and sesame seeds for a marinade.
2. Marinate the fish fillets in the marinade for at least 2 hours.
3. Place fillets in the broiler; pour a little of the sauce over them and broil 4 minutes.
4. Turn fillets over, sprinkle with more of the marinade, and cover lightly with the sesame seeds.
5. Broil until done, being careful not to overcook.

This dish of Rako's is very unusual. It's always fun to surprise guests with it.

gingami yaki

1   small fish fillet per person
1   tbsp. sake per person (rice wine)
Salt and pepper, to taste
2   whole shrimp per person
1   large mushroom per person
Peanut or sesame seed oil
1   can Ginko nuts (found in oriental shops, or substitute a can of kumquats)

1.   Sprinkle each piece of fish with 1 tbsp. sake and a little bit of salt and pepper, and let stand for 15 minutes.
2.   Remove legs and tip of tail from shrimp.
3.   Make a cut along back of shell with a sharp knife and remove vein with a toothpick.
4.   Make a lot of tiny slits in the mushroom cap and cut off stem.
5.   Take a small rectangle of foil for each person and brush lightly with oil.
6.   On each piece of foil place one shrimp, one fillet, one mushroom cap, and a few nuts or kumquats.
7.   Fold foil in the shape of a boat, making sure all ingredients are covered.
8.   Place "boats" in a frying pan over medium heat, cover and bake 10 to 15 minutes, depending on thickness of fillets and size of shrimp.

florence grey's fish with hot sauce

4   large scallions
2   tbsp. fresh ginger, minced
1   tbsp. butter
3/4 cup white wine
1/2 tsp. Chinese chili paste
4   fish fillets (approximately 1/2 lb. each)
Safflower oil (for brushing fillets)

1.   Cut the scallions into 1-inch pieces; then slice vertically into very thin strips.
2.   Saute scallions and ginger in butter, stirring lightly.
3.   Add wine and cook over low heat until the wine has evaporated slightly (about 5 minutes).
4.   Add 1/2 tsp. chili paste and stir well.
5.   Check for spiciness, adding more if needed. (Chinese chili paste is very hot.)
6.   Brush fillets lightly with oil and broil.
7.   Spoon chili sauce over each fillet and serve immediately.

Bernice Hunt's salmon mousse is really not difficult to make, nor is it fattening. It is an impressive dish to serve—very light and delicate.

bernice's easy salmon mousse

2 6-oz. cans of salmon or equivalent amount of poached salmon, bones and skin removed
1 envelope plain gelatin
1/4 cup cold water
1/2 cup boiling water
1/2 cup mayonnaise
1 tbsp. lemon juice
1 tsp. grated onion
1/2 tsp. Tabasco
1 tsp. salt
1 tbsp capers, chopped
1½ cups cottage cheese
Salad greens, for garnish

1. Prepare salmon by draining and flaking it, being sure to remove skin and bones.
2. Soften gelatin in cold water; then dissolve it in the boiling water.
3. Add gelatin to salmon; then stir in mayonnaise, lemon juice, onion, Tabasco, salt, and chopped capers.
4. Whip cottage cheese in blender until smooth and creamy.
5. Combine cottage cheese with salmon and the other ingredients; blend.
6. Pour into a 1½ quart mold that has been lightly oiled.
7. Chill until set.
8. When ready to serve, unmold on a bed of salad greens.

This is another one of those Indiana dishes. It can be used as a main dish, an appetizer, or a salad.

christine's shrimp salad

1/2 lb. shrimp, cleaned, cooked and diced
1 cup celery, diced
1 cup onions, diced
2 tbsp. olive oil
1/4 cup lemon juice
Salt and pepper, to taste
Lettuce, for garnish

1. Combine shrimp, celery and onions and coat well with olive oil.
2. Add lemon juice, salt, and pepper, and mix.
3. Chill and serve on a bed of crisp lettuce.

This comes from Marty's cousin Cynthia. By the time I first tasted it, I already had all my recipes, but there was so much enthusiasm for this one that I had to include it. Her recipe fed at least 12 people. For a family dinner, I cut it in half.

You can use all kinds of substitutions—striped bass for the weakfish, clams instead of mussels. Experiment! But remember to buy fish that is not too thin or it will flake too easily and disappear into the sauce.

east hampton cioppino

3   fat cloves garlic
2   onions, cut into rings
1/4 cup olive oil
2   tbsp. curry powder
2   weakfish, cut into steaks (4-5 lbs.)
1   cup dry white wine
2   bay leaves
1   2-lb. can Italian plum tomatoes
3   lbs. mussels, cleaned
1   lb. scallops
1   cup parsley, chopped

1. Flatten garlic with a cleaver
2. Saute onion and garlic in olive oil until golden.
3. Add curry powder and cook 2 minutes.
4. Push onion aside and brown fish steaks until barely brown.
5. Remove fish from pan and set aside.
6. Add wine to the onion and garlic in pan.
7. Add bay leaves and canned tomatoes to pan and simmer gently until slightly reduced. (To this point, everything can be done well in advance.)
8. Return fish steaks to broth and simmer until fish is almost opaque.
9. Add mussels and scallops; cover and steam until mussels have opened.
10. Toss parsley over stew and serve.

My stepmother, Fern, comes from Nebraska and is an excellent cook. What has always impressed me is that, penny-for-penny, she is probably the most economical cook I know. Without resorting to filet mignon, fancy sauces or accompaniments from the gourmet shops, she prepares food which is always superb. This is one of her simplest dishes.

fern's tuna paprika

2   tsp. butter
1   clove garlic, peeled
1   medium onion, chopped
1/2 medium green pepper, seeded and
      chopped
2   6½-oz. cans tuna
2   tbsp. paprika
1   cup sour cream
2   tbsp. sherry
2   cans Chinese noodles

1. Melt butter in skillet and saute garlic for a minute.
2. Add onion and pepper to skillet and saute over low heat for three minutes.
3. Drain tuna and chop in another bowl.
4. Add paprika and sour cream and mix well.
5. Add tuna mixture to sauteed onion and pepper; stir and heat thoroughly.
6. Serve over Chinese noodles.

My husband Marty concocted this. It's pretty foolproof and an easy meal when you're having company. Garnish with more parsley and scallions, if you wish. This dish is good as a leftover, served cold. The sauce jells in the refrigerator and may be served as "fish in aspic."

fish with soy sauce

4   large scallions
2   large cloves garlic, minced
3   tsp. fresh ginger, grated
4   tbsp. fresh parsley, finely chopped
1   tbsp. safflower oil
1/2 cup soy sauce
Juice of one lemon
6   fish fillets

1. Slice scallion tops into 1-inch pieces; then sliver.

2. Saute garlic, ginger, scallions, and parsley in oil for 3 minutes, stirring frequently.
3. Add soy sauce and the juice of one lemon and cook over low heat for 15 minutes.
4. Place fish in large baking dish, making sure that the pieces don't overlap.
5. Cover with sauce and bake at 350 degrees, covering fish until done. This can take 20 to 30 minutes, depending on the thickness of the fish.

This is a recipe that I probably first had out in Indiana and I am including it for children everywhere. It's simple, inexpensive, and my children used to request it at least once a week. My stepchildren then took up the requests and pretty soon all the neighborhood children were asking me to write it down for their mothers. So, somehow, it seemed right to include it, even though it could not be considered gourmet cooking in any way, shape, or form. You may want to use more or less milk, depending on how thick you like the sauce.

all children's favorite "tuna on rice"

2   6½-oz cans tuna, drained (I prefer the chunk light tuna.)
1   can mushroom soup (Purists can make their own)
1   cup milk
1   tbsp. Worcestershire sauce
Garlic salt, to taste
Pepper, to taste
4   cups cooked rice

1. In a heavy saucepan, chop up tuna.
2. Add mushroom soup and mix well.
3. Add milk, Worcestershire, a sprinkling of garlic salt and pepper.
4. Cook over low heat for about 15 minutes.
5. Serve over cooked rice.

meat

meat

What can I say about meat? I really try not to have too much of it, so when I do, I want each dish to be special. I also notice that both my husband and I seem to crave meat more in cold weather, so I have to be a little more watchful then of our menus, serving more "hearty" dishes as a substitute.

When Marty and I went to Argentina some years ago, we became friends with a very handsome doctor and psychiatrist. Don Mathews speaks with an impeccable English accent, writes poetry, is very dashing, and we wish he didn't live so far away. He visited us in Bridgehampton about five years ago and insisted one night on making a stew for a large gathering of friends. We were glad that he did. It's a splendid dish for a snowy night. Although he used fresh pumpkin chunks, I used squash at Dorothy Friedman's suggestion. Pumpkin is in season for such a short time, and canned pumpkin just won't do.

Don says the meat can be marinated in wine, bayleaf, oregano, salt, and pepper if you wish. And you may also add peeled, halved, pears for an even richer stew.

don mathews' "carbonada criolla"

2   tbsp. oil
2   lbs. lean beef, cut into bite-sized pieces
3   bay leaves
1/2 tsp. pepper
4   large potatoes, peeled and quartered
4   sweet potatoes, peeled and halved
8   medium onions, peeled and halved
4   tbsp. oregano
1/2 tsp. salt
1   large acorn squash (or one small pumpkin)
Corn on the cob (½ cob for each person)
12 peach halves (fresh are nicer, canned will do)

1. In a large, heavy stewing pot, heat the oil and, when hot, brown the meat quickly with 1 bay leaf and the pepper.
2. Turn heat to low, cover, and add both kinds of potatoes, the onions, the other two bay leaves and 1 cup water.
3. Sprinkle with oregano and salt; cover and cook over low heat for 1/2 hour.
4. Peel and seed the squash and cut into large chunks. If you use pumpkin, there is no need to peel it.
5. Husk corn if you're using fresh corn. Either way, break the corn cobs in half.
6. After the meat has cooked for a half hour, add the squash or pumpkin, corn, and peaches. (If using fresh peaches, they should be peeled.)
7. Cook 1/4 hour more or until the meat and vegetables are tender.
8. Serve in large soup bowls with French bread and wine.

When I was in college, I had a Greek boyfriend and, often, when I ate at his family's home, we were served "dolmades." Later, as a young newlywed, this became my party recipe. When my children arrived, it became a favorite of theirs probably because they were enchanted with wrapping these small packages, eating a lot of the leaves along the way. I still think it's a very special dish. It is helpful to have someone assist you when you are ready to make the sauce, and then it must be eaten immediately.

I realize all this sounds like quite a job, but, once you get the hang of it, it's not that bad, and definitely worth it. Besides, small children make wonderful "rollers."

my dolmades

1   lb. ground sirloin
1   medium onion, minced
1   cup uncooked white rice
1/2 tsp. cinnamon
Salt and pepper, to taste
2   cups canned tomatoes
1   jar Greek grape leaves packed in brine (available in any specialty shop, and often in supermarkets)

1. In a mixing bowl, combine the meat, onion, rice, cinnamon, salt and pepper.
2. Squeeze the juice from the tomatoes and add them to the meat mixture, mixing well with your hands.
3. Drain the grape leaves.
4. Place a small amount of meat in the center of each grape leaf, wrapping as you go. (The leaves are of different sizes, so you won't always put in the same amount of meat. However, you don't want any huge rolls; they should be somewhat uniform in size.)

5. To wrap dolmades, fold the top of the leaf over the meat, then the two sides, then roll the leaf down to catch the bottom. If that sounds a little confusing, here's a diagram that should help.

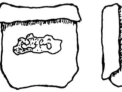

6. Place each roll snugly in a medium-sized pot. When the bottom is covered, start a second row and continue layering.
7. Add 3 cups water; then place a heavy plate or lid directly on top of dolmades to keep them in place while cooking.
8. Cook over low heat for one hour, adding more water if needed. After cooking, you should have about two cups of broth for making the sauce.
(See next page for Avgolemono sauce)

avgolemono sauce

4 eggs
Hot broth from the dolmades
Juice from two lemons

1. Beat eggs in a large bowl until they are nice and frothy.
2. Very slowly pour the hot broth into the eggs, making sure the dolmades don't slip out. This is where you should have someone help, as you should continue beating the eggs while an assistant pours the broth.
3. Add the lemon juice and stir. If you like things very tart, you may want to add more lemon.
4. Pour sauce back over the dolmades and serve immediately.

Argentina has such marvelous beef! You really need to buy a choice cut to approximate it. This dish was served to us by one of our friends who lives there and I've never come across a recipe like it here in the States.

argentine steak

Steak fillets, sirloin (enough for 4)
4 egg yolks
1½ cups sifted flour
1/2 cup milk
1 clove garlic, minced
1½ tsp. salt
1/2 tsp. pepper
1/2 tsp. marjoram
4 egg whites
4 tbsp. safflower oil

1. Trim all fat and bone from meat and cut into serving pieces.
2. Beat egg yolks; then gradually stir in flour until smooth.
3. Add milk, garlic, salt, pepper, and marjoram; beat until you have a smooth mixture.
4. Whip egg whites until they form soft peaks.
5. Fold egg whites into egg-flour mixture.
6. Dip steak into batter.
7. Fry, turning once, in hot oil until done. (Cooking time will depend on the thickness of the steak and whether you like it rare, medium, or well done.)

After existing on lots of meat loaves in the early years of my marriage, I never thought I'd want to make another one. But Jeanne Humphries convinced me otherwise when she brought this to another of our communal dancing and drumming sessions.

jeanne humphries's juicy meatloaf

2   lbs. ground chuck
2   onions, 1 large, 1 small (chopped fine)
1   small green pepper, diced (seeds and stems removed)
2   eggs, beaten
3/4 tsp. paprika
2   cloves garlic, chopped (or 1/2 tsp. garlic powder)
Salt and pepper to taste
1   6-oz. can tomato sauce
1   tbsp. catsup
1   tbsp. soy sauce
1   tsp. Worcestershire sauce
1/2 tsp. chili powder (more if you like a spicy sauce)
1/2 tsp. garlic powder
1   small onion

1. Combine meat with the large chopped onion, green pepper, 2 beaten eggs, paprika, garlic, salt, and pepper.
2. Mix thoroughly and shape into loaf.
3. Place in small roasting pan.
4. Combine tomato sauce, catsup, soy sauce, Worcestershire sauce, chili powder, garlic powder and small, chopped onion. Add salt and pepper to taste.
5. Mix thoroughly and pour over meatloaf.
6. Bake for 1 hour and 5 minutes in a 350-degree oven.

This is another recipe from my Greek friends in Silver Spring.

greek meatballs

1   lb. ground chuck or ground round
1   medium onion, chopped fine
1   egg
1/2 cup bread crumbs
1   tsp. anise seeds
1   tsp. salt
3/4 tsp. pepper
2   tbsp. cooking oil
1   small (6-oz.) can tomato paste

1. Mix meat, onion, egg, bread crumbs, anise seeds, 1/2 tsp. of the salt, and 1/4 tsp. of the pepper.
2. Oil hands lightly with salad oil and shape mixture into tiny meatballs. Bessie Ahouris said that oiling your hands makes it easier to roll the meatballs.
3. Brown meatballs quickly on all sides in a hot pan. (If you use ground chuck, you probably won't have to add any oil. If you use ground round, add 2 tbsp. oil.
5. Mix 1 can of tomato paste with 3 cans of water, the rest of the salt (1/2 tsp.) and pepper (1/2 tsp.).
6. Transfer meatballs to a pot and pour sauce over them.
7. Simmer, covered, for 45 minutes.

This is another of Armand LaMacchia's recipes. Armand does everything well but, of course, he has a special knack for Italian cooking!

armand's veal

8   slices of veal, very thin and from a good
      cut
3   lemons
1/2 cup flour
1/3 stick butter
Salt and pepper, to taste

1. Pound veal slices as thin as possible with a wooden mallet.
2. Squeeze two of the lemons; slice the other into thin rounds and put aside.
3. Dust each slice of veal lightly in flour on both sides.
4. Melt butter over medium heat and fry veal for just a few moments, turning once.
5. Place veal on platter and pour the lemon juice over it.
6. Sprinkle with salt and pepper and arrange lemon slices on top.

Our friend Craig brought a Swedish girlfriend out to visit at our beach house. A tall, pretty woman who laughed easily, Barbara surprised me by forfeiting time on the beach to cook us a Swedish meal. Here are her meatballs, and in the dessert section, you'll see what she baked for us.

barbara's swedish meatballs

1   large potato
1   cup bread crumbs
1/2 cup milk
1   lb. ground pork
1/3 lb. ground beef
1   medium onion, chopped
1   clove garlic, minced
1   tsp. salt
1/2 tsp. pepper
2   eggs

1. Peel potato, cook in boiling water and mash.
2. Soak bread crumbs in milk and squeeze out excess liquid.
3. Combine meat, mashed potato, onion, garlic, bread crumbs, salt, pepper, and eggs and mix well.
4. Shape into large meatballs.
5. Brown over high heat, turning on all sides.
6. Lower heat and cook meatballs until done, turning frequently so they don't stick.

My grandmother had bright red hair, was called "Honey," and sang "Good Morning Merry Sunshine" to me every morning. I have cherished memories of marvelous picnics with her in the back yard, a yard framed with lilacs, old fashioned flower gardens, and even bleeding hearts. This was one of her picnic specials and everyone made his own portion.

honey's kebabs

1½ lbs. beef (a good cut for broiling, such
    as sirloin tip, London broil, etc.)
3   tbsp. oil
2   tbsp. vinegar
1/4 tsp. garlic salt
1/4 tsp. pepper
2   large green peppers
12 small pearl onions
1/4 lb. bacon
24 cherry tomatoes
12 large mushrooms

1. Trim all fat from meat and cut into bite-sized pieces.
2. Marinate meat in a mixture of oil, vinegar, garlic salt, and pepper for 1 to 2 hours.
3. Seed green peppers and cut into pieces large enough to be threaded on a skewer without breaking
4. Skin onions and leave whole.
5. Cut bacon into small pieces. (I think today I would probably omit the bacon unless I bought some without the nitrates.)
6. Arrange meat, green pepper, onions, bacon, tomatoes, and mushrooms in separate bowls.
7. Alternate meat with the bacon and vegetables on skewers.
8. Cook in broiler or over charcoal, turning occasionally, until done (Take special care that the bacon is done.)
9. Serve on rice or in rolls, if you wish, for a perfect picnic.

This is another one from Pauline Gomez, and a great way to make your own kind of chow mein. It is very important, if you are using frozen peapods, to extract every bit of water from them. Otherwise your chow mein will taste watery.

pauline's chow mein

1½ lbs. flank steak or sirloin tip
1/4 cup sherry
1/2 cup soy sauce
2   cups fresh bamboo shoots *or*
1   8-oz. can bamboo shoots
1   8-oz. can water chestnuts
3   tbsp. oil
2   cloves garlic, minced
2   6-oz. boxes peapods (or even better, fresh ones)

1. Cut meat in very thin, diagonal strips of uniform length (from 2 to 4 inches).
2. Mix sherry and soy sauce and marinate the meat in it for 1/2 hour.
3. Drain and rinse bamboo shoots if using canned ones.
4. Drain and cut chestnuts into small matchlike strips.
5. Drain meat, reserving any marinade, and heat oil in wok.
6. Cook garlic and ginger in hot oil for 1 to 2 minutes.
7. Add meat and stir fry until done. (This should take only a couple of minutes.)
8. Add bamboo shoots, chestnuts, and peapods; stir fry for 2 to 3 minutes more.
9. Add the leftover marinade to wok, giving it a few minutes to heat; serve immediately.

This is a recipe that I experimented with and adapted after having something similar at various Thai restaurants.

thailand beef salad

1½ lbs. beef (top round, sirloin, etc.)
5   tbsp. oil
3   tbsp. soy sauce
1   head romaine
1/2 cup fish sauce or stock (see note)
1/2 to 1 tsp. hot red pepper
1   cucumber, peeled and thinly sliced
2   tomatoes, cut into eighths
8 to 12 radishes, thinly sliced
1   red onion, thinly sliced
1   bunch scallions, cut into 1-inch pieces
1   tsp. basil
1   tsp. mint
Salt and pepper, to taste

1. Slice beef in very thin diagonal strips, 3 to 4 inches in length, and marinate in 3 tbsp. of the oil and the soy sauce for a couple of hours.
2. Break romaine into bite-sized pieces.
3. Cook fish sauce or stock with the red pepper for 10 minutes over low heat.
4. Put cucumber, tomatoes, radishes, onion, and scallions into salad bowl with the romaine, basil, mint, salt, and pepper; toss briefly.
5. Drain meat.
6. Heat wok with remaining 2 tbsp. oil; add meat, and stir fry until done (just a few minutes, until meat loses its rawness.)
7. Add meat immediately to salad and pour hot pepper sauce over it.
8. Mix and serve.

Note: You can buy prepared fish sauce at an oriental store, make your own fish broth, or simply use beef broth.

This is another dish from my Japanese friend, Rako. It's extremely good and happens to look very pretty when it's served. She called it "Sammi Yaki."

sammi yaki

1 lb. lean pork
1 scallion
2 tbsp. sesame seeds
2 tbsp. soy sauce
2 tbsp. sake (rice wine)
1 small red pepper, sliced into matchlike strips
1 tsp. pepper
2 tbsp. vinegar (preferably rice vinegar or cider vinegar)
1 tsp. sugar
3 tbsp. oil
1 box Japanese noodles, or very thin vermicelli
1 small cucumber, peeled and cut into thin strips
1 tomato, cut into small chunks

1. Slice pork in thin diagonal strips, making sure to trim off all the fat.
2. Slice the scallion lengthwise and then into 1-inch pieces.
3. Marinate the meat in a sauce made from the sesame seeds, soy sauce, sake, scallion, and red pepper strips for one hour.
4. Make a pepper sauce from the pepper, vinegar, and sugar. Set aside.
5. Heat oil in heavy skillet or wok and stir fry meat and red peppers quickly until done. Make sure you have drained off all the marinade. Keep warm.
6. Cook noodles according to directions and drain.
7. Mix noodles with cucumber and tomatoes.
8. Put noodles in a serving dish, place meat and peppers on top and pour the pepper sauce over it.

poultry

poultry

Chicken is such a versatile bird and there are so many recipes. I have tried to select the most tempting, those that are really exemplary. I suppose there is really nothing better than a good roast chicken with a stuffing, but when you have chicken fairly often, it's pleasant to surprise yourself.

vincenzo's chicken

4   tbsp. butter
4   tbsp. oil
3   cloves garlic, sliced
1/2 tsp. basil
1/2 tsp. rosemary
1/4 tsp. red pepper
1   chicken, cut into small frying pieces
4   fresh tomatoes, skinned
1   cup white wine
1/4 tsp. nutmeg
1/2 tsp. salt
1/4 tsp. pepper

1. Melt butter and oil and saute garlic until lightly browned.
2. Add basil, rosemary, and red pepper; cook 1 minute.
3. Add chicken and brown over medium heat.
4. Cut tomatoes into quarters and add to chicken.
5. Add white wine, nutmeg, and sprinkle with salt and pepper.
6. Cover and cook in oven for approximately 1 hour at 350 degrees.

Note: Vincenzo says that he prefers to use a clay pot for oven cooking.

Bill Kaukeano is a huge, gentle man from Hawaii. He's as curious as a child and has traveled many paths in the course of a very interesting life. He loves to cook for his friends and I have a fond memory of him cooking for a large group of us on a tiny hibachi on his New York City fire escape. This is a different recipe of his, just as good.

bill's hawaiian chicken

3/4 cup catsup
1/4 cup honey
1/2 cup apple vinegar
1   cup soy sauce
3   tsp. mustard
2   cloves garlic, minced
2   tbsp. raw ginger, grated
1   chicken, cut into individual pieces

1. Combine all ingredients, except the chicken, and mix well.
2. Marinate chicken pieces in this sauce for two hours.
3. Place chicken in an ovenproof dish with the marinade, cover, and bake at 350 degrees until done (1 to 1½ hours).

My aunt Peg is from New England and says "ayeh" when the rest of us say "yes," "well," or "oh." I haven't seen her in quite a while and she will probably be surprised to see her recipe in my book; I had it at her house such a long time ago. I like it because it can be prepared in advance, then just popped into the oven after work, or for company. I suppose you could even freeze it and have it on hand.

aunt peg's chicken and broccoli casserole

4   chicken breasts
2   onions, coarsely chopped
1   carrot, coarsely chopped
1/2 tsp. salt
1/4 tsp. pepper
2   tbsp. butter
2   tsp. flour
1½ cups milk
1½ cups sharp cheddar cheese, grated
1   head broccoli
1/2 cup bread crumbs

1. Stew chicken breasts in 2 cups water with the onions, carrot, salt and pepper.
2. When cooked, remove meat from chicken and reserve, discarding skin and bones. (Save broth for soup.)
3. Melt butter in a pan; add flour and stir.
4. Gradually add milk to make a smooth sauce.
5. Add grated cheese, a little at a time; continue stirring until you have a smooth cheese sauce.
6. Cut broccoli into lengthwise pieces, removing leaves and tough ends of stems.
7. Steam broccoli until done, but not at all mushy. (Broccoli should have a certain crispness.)
8. Place chicken and drained broccoli in layers in a flameproof casserole.
9. Pour cheese sauce over casserole and sprinkle with the bread crumbs.
10. Place foil over dish and bake at 350 degrees for 1 hour.
11. Remove foil and place dish under the broiler for a few minutes so that the cheese sauce bubbles and becomes slightly brown.

I remember my daughter, Liza, at age thirteen, cooking a huge dinner for about twelve of us. Not only did she accomplish this in under two hours, but she also managed to produce a flaky, rich apple pie. Pigtails flying, she whizzed around the kitchen and astounded all of us with her feast. Liza, at 13 years, used frozen vegetables, but you can substitute fresh ones.

liza's chicken potpourri

1 frying chicken, cut in pieces
4 tbsp. butter
1 medium onion, chopped
4 tomatoes, quartered
1 cup chicken broth
1/2 tsp. thyme
1/2 tsp. basil
Salt and pepper, to taste
1 10-oz. package frozen baby lima beans
1 10-oz. package frozen corn

1. Brown chicken in butter and then place in dutch oven (deep pot with lid).
2. Saute chopped onion in same butter, then add to chicken.
3. Add tomatoes, broth, thyme, basil, salt, and pepper; cover and simmer over low heat for 45 minutes.
4. Add frozen vegetables and simmer 20 minutes more, until done.

pauline's hoisin chicken

4 double chicken breasts, boned and cut into bite-sized pieces
2 tsp. cornstarch
1/4 cup (plus 1 tbsp.) light soy sauce (found in Chinese markets)
1 cup dried Chinese mushrooms
2 tbsp. oil
1 package peapods (or fresh ones, if available)
1 tbsp. dark soy sauce
1 tbsp. dry sherry
2 tbsp. Hoisin Sauce (found in Chinese markets).

1. Sprinkle chicken pieces with cornstarch and soak in 1/4 cup light soy sauce for about 20 minutes.
2. Soak mushrooms in warm water for 15 minutes; then remove the tough center nubs.
3. Heat the oil in a wok and stir fry mushrooms and peapods for 2 minutes.
4. Remove vegetables, add chicken to wok and stir fry until it is no longer pink. (You may have to add more oil.)
5. Return vegetables to wok.
6. Add the 1 tbsp. light soy sauce, 1 tbsp. dark soy sauce, sherry, and the Hoisin Sauce; stir fry for 1 minute to mix, then serve immediately.

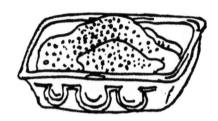

I mentioned Gay Tarlo earlier because she is the wife of Bill Tarlo who has promised me his secret curry recipe for years. Gay also has a secret recipe for chicken. She was paid the highest compliment on it by my two teenage stepsons, Marc and Richard, who told her that "It's better than anything at McDonald's." This is included for the pleasure of all teenage boys, and also because it's very good.

gay's secret chicken recipe

1   cup flour
1/2 tsp. salt
4   tsp. black pepper
2   tsp. powdered ginger
2   tsp. coriander
2   tbsp. paprika
2   eggs
3   tbsp. frozen orange juice concentrate (undiluted)
4   cups corn flakes from the health store or health food shelves of your super-market
1   frying chicken, cut in pieces
3/4 stick butter

1. Mix flour, salt, pepper, ginger, coriander and paprika in a paper bag.
2. Beat the eggs with 2 tbsp. cold water; add to frozen orange juice concentrate.
3. Crush the cereal into fine crumbs.
4. Dip each piece of chicken in the egg mixture; then coat with crumbs.
5. Arrange chicken in a lightly oiled roasting pan; pieces should lie flat, not heaped on top of each other.
6. Melt butter and drizzle over chicken.
7. Bake, uncovered, at 325 degrees for 1½ to 2 hours.

This is a recipe using the same basic mix as her baked chicken, but with some additions. Gay recommends a lot of freshly-ground black pepper, and I remember her chicken was nicely hot, so you may want to add more pepper.

gay's secret roast chicken

1   roasting chicken (about 6 lbs.)
1   lemon
1   small orange
1   heel of bread
2   tsp. powdered ginger
2   tsp. coriander
2   tbsp. paprika
2   tbsp. black pepper
2   tbsp. frozen orange juice concentrate (undiluted)
1/2 cup mustard sauce (See last chapter for recipe.)
3/4 stick butter

1.   Clean chicken and squeeze the juice of the lemon inside the chicken cavity.
2.   Place the squeezed lemon inside the cavity along with the orange.
3.   Close the cavity with a heel of bread.
4.   Make a mixture of the ginger, coriander, paprika, pepper, and orange juice concentrate.
5.   Mix it with the mustard and spread evenly over the chicken.
6.   Melt butter and drizzle over the chicken.
7.   Cover with foil and bake in a roasting pan for 3 to 4 hours at 325 degrees, or until chicken is done. Take the foil off for the last 20 minutes. Baste often so it is nicely browned and skin does not become dry.

armand's chicken wings

8   chicken wings (at least 2 per person)
2   cups chicken broth
1   medium onion, finely chopped
Salt and pepper, to taste
1/2 tsp. garlic powder
2   tbsp. fresh parsley, finely chopped
1½ tbsp. paprika
1   cup duck sauce (brands such as Saucy Susan contain no preservatives or artificial additives.)

1. Wash chicken wings thoroughly and place in a baking dish, so that the chicken pieces don't overlap.
2. Add chicken broth to pan, making sure that there's at least 1/2 inch in the bottom of the pan.
3. Add chopped onion.

4. Sprinkle wings with salt, pepper, 1/4 tsp. of the garlic powder, 1 tbsp. of the parsley, and half of the paprika.
5. Bake, uncovered, at 400 degrees for 1/2 hour.
6. Turn wings over and sprinkle with more salt and pepper and the rest of the parsley and spices; bake in oven for 10 minutes more.
7. Remove wings and place on broiler, underside up.
8. Cover with 1/2 cup of the duck sauce and broil for five minutes.
9. Turn wings over; add the other 1/2 cup of the sauce and broil five minutes more. (You can use more duck sauce, if necessary.)

This last recipe is an adaptation from a well-known chef. The chef's recipe seemed so long and difficult to follow that I changed it around to something I could handle.

herbed chicken

1   frying chicken, cut in pieces
Salt and pepper, to taste
3   tbsp. butter
3/4 cup white wine
2   tbsp. parsley
2   tbsp. chives
1   tbsp. tarragon
1   tbsp. chervil
1/2 tsp. thyme

1. Rub chicken with salt and pepper and brown in butter.
2. Add 1/2 cup of the wine and cook for 10 minutes over medium heat.
3. Add remaining wine and the herbs.
4. Cover pan, turn heat to low, and cook until tender. Simple!!

desserts

desserts

I don't make too many desserts because I don't like to eat too much sugar and my family is capable of overdosing on sweets. Also, by the time I finish cooking everything else, I often don't have much time left. When I do serve them, I prefer desserts that are very simple. Fruit and cheese are probably my all-time favorites—no time and no fuss. However, an indulgence is very nice once in a while. So, here are a few.

I believe Mrs. Knudson is a "very distant relative." I'm not even sure of that, but these have been in my recipe files for years. Cooks probably already know this, but my grandmother always said the best way to tell if baked goods are done is to stick a toothpick in the middle. If it comes out clean, it's ready.

mrs. knudson's carrot cake

3   cups flour
2   cups raw sugar
2   tsp. baking powder
2   tsp. cinnamon
1/4 tsp. salt
2   cups carrots, grated
1½ cups safflower oil
1   cup chopped nuts
1   cup coconut
2   tsp. vanilla
1   small can crushed pineapple (approximately 8 oz.)
3   eggs

1. Mix all dry ingredients.
2. Add remaining ingredients and mix well.
3. Bake in an ungreased angel food or loaf pan for 1 hour at 350 degrees.
    Easy!

mrs. knudson's pumpkin bread

3   cups brown sugar (no lumps)
4   eggs, beaten
1   cup safflower oil
2   cups pumpkin puree
3½ cups sifted flour
1   tsp. baking soda
2   tsp. baking powder
2   tsp. salt
2   tsp. cinnamon
1   tsp. allspice
1   tsp. powdered cloves
2/3 cup water
1/2 to 3/4 cup chopped nuts

1. Combine brown sugar with eggs and mix well.
2. Add oil and mix again.
3. Stir in pumpkin puree.
4. Add all dry ingredients and mix thoroughly.
5. Add nuts and stir.
6. Pour into two lightly greased loaf pans.
7. Bake at 350 degrees until done (approximately 45 minutes to 1 hour).

This is one of my mother-in-law's desserts. When she had her own garden with fruit trees, she used fresh blueberries or apples. If you can't find the fresh fruit, used canned or frozen, but fresh is best.

marcia's kuchen

1½ cups unbleached flour
2   tsp. baking powder
1/4 tsp. salt
1/2 cup shortening or butter
1   cup raw sugar
3   eggs
1   tsp. vanilla
3 to 4 cups apples, peeled and sliced, or
     blueberries, or pitted cherries

1. Sift flour, baking powder, and salt together.
2. Cream shortening or butter with sugar.
3. Add eggs and vanilla to shortening and sugar and mix.
4. Add dry ingredients that have been sifted, and mix.
5. Grease and flour a square baking pan.
6. Spread dough in pan. (It will be sticky.)
7. Add the fruit, spreading to cover dough; press it in firmly.
8. Crumble the following topping over fruit and bake at 350 degrees for 45 minutes.

Crumb Topping

1/3 cup raw sugar
1/2 cup unbleached flour
1/2 stick softened butter

1. Mix flour and sugar.
2. Cut butter into mixture.

This is the dessert that my Swedish acquaintance, Barbara, made when she prepared her Swedish meatballs. It's easier than apple pie and I happen to like it more.

barbara's apple tarte

1   stick soft butter
1   cup sugar
1   egg
2   cups flour, sifted
1½ tsp. baking powder, sifted
3   cups apples, peeled and sliced
6   tbsp. sugar
2   tbsp. cinnamon

1. Take a tiny piece of the butter and grease a shallow baking dish or pie tin.
2. Mix the rest of the butter with sugar.

3. Add the egg and stir.
4. Add flour and baking powder; stir and let mixture stand for half an hour.
5. Mix apples with sugar and cinnamon.
6. Take flour mixture and press it into a pie plate with fingers, leaving out 1/4 of mixture for top of tarte.
7. Spread apples over pie crust and sprinkle the remaining flour mix on top.
8. Bake at 350 degrees for 40 minutes or until done.

my cheesecake

20 pieces melba toast
9   tbsp. raw sugar
2   tbsp. fresh wheat germ
1/3 cup melted butter
1   tsp. vanilla
1   lb. cream cheese
4   tbsp. sifted, unbleached flour
1/4 tsp. salt
4   eggs separated
1   tbsp. lemon juice
3/4 cup half-and-half cream

1. Whirl melba toast in a blender or crush with a rolling pin to make crumbs.
2. Mix the crumbs with 1 tbsp. of the sugar and the wheat germ.

3. Add melted butter to crumb mixture and mix thoroughly.
4. Press crumbs into a 9-inch pie plate.
5. Add vanilla to cream cheese and mix.
6. Add 4 tbsp. sugar, flour, and salt; cream until the cheese mixture is light and fluffy.
7. Beat egg yolks and add along with the lemon juice and the cream.
8. Beat egg whites until thick; then add the remaining 4 tbsp. sugar, one at a time.
9. Fold egg whites into the cream cheese mixture.
10. Pour filling into the pie crust and bake at 350 degrees for about 1½ hours, or until done.

Pam Topham is a weaver who designs and makes beautiful wall hangings. I'm always fascinated by her workroom with its imposing loom and baskets of gaily colored yarn. Besides all that, she makes wonderful succulent desserts. This is one that I like because it is so easy and quick to prepare.

pam's easy delicious

1   pint whipping cream
1/4 cup raw sugar (This will not blend as well as refined sugar, but I still use it.)
Any fresh fruit, sliced (bananas, apples, berries, peaches, pears, melon, etc.) in combination with a handful of nuts, such as slivered almonds, pine nuts, walnuts, etc.

1. Whip cream and, when thickened, add sugar a little at a time.
2. Combine whipped cream with fruit and nuts and serve.

These four desserts of mine are all easy to make and take very little time, which is what I seem to be looking for after preparing the main dishes.

easy baked custard

1/2 cup raw sugar
1/2 cup milk powder
Dash of salt
3   eggs
1/2 cup fresh milk
1/2 tsp. vanilla
1½ cups reconstituted dry milk (dry milk mixed with the appropriate amount of water)
Nutmeg

1. Mix sugar, milk powder and salt.
2. Beat eggs and add to dry ingredients.

3. Add fresh milk and vanilla.
4. Add the reconstituted dry milk and stir well.
5. Pour into a baking dish that has been lightly coated with cooking oil.
6. Sprinkle with nutmeg.
7. Bake in 350-degree oven until done (approximately 1 hour).

Note: I usually place the custard dish in a pan with a small amount of water in the bottom to prevent burning. When a knife, inserted in the middle of the custard, comes out clean, the custard is ready.

a special yogurt dessert

1/2 lb. seedless grapes
1/4 to 1/2 cup nuts, slivered, or broken
    into small pieces
2   cups yogurt
1 to 2 tbsp. honey (optional)

1. Leave grapes whole or slice them in half. (I prefer them sliced, but it takes a little more time.)
2. Add nuts and yogurt; mix.
3. Add honey to sweeten, if desired.
4. Chill before serving.

broiled grapefruit

2   grapefruits
4   tbsp. brown or raw sugar
4   tbsp. liquor (rum, Cointreau, etc.)

1. Slice grapefruits in half and loosen the sections.
2. Sprinkle sugar and liquor on top.
3. Broil for a couple of minutes in broiler and serve warm.

bananas cardamom

4   bananas
4   tbsp. butter
1   tbsp. sugar
1   tsp. cardamom
1   tbsp. lemon juice

1. Peel bananas and slice lengthwise.
2. Melt butter over low heat in frying pan.
3. Add bananas to pan.
4. Sprinkle with sugar, cardamom and lemon juice and cook for about five minutes.
5. Turn bananas over to coat; cook a few minutes more and serve.

This is from the Greeks again. It's very rich and is used on special occasions.

karethopita

1   lb. chopped walnuts
1   box Zweiback
1   dozen eggs
2   cups raw sugar
2   tsp. baking powder
2   tsp. nutmeg
1   jigger whiskey or brandy

1. Grind walnuts in blender into small pieces or crumbs; put in mixing bowl.
2. Grind Zweiback in blender to fine crumbs and add to walnuts.
3. Separate egg yolks and whirl them with sugar in a blender for 2 or 3 minutes.

4. Add baking powder, nutmeg, whiskey or brandy and mix well with walnut mixture.
5. Add sugar and egg mixture to bowl and stir well.
6. In a separate bowl, beat egg whites until stiff.
7. Fold egg whites into other ingredients.
8. Pour into large rectangular Pyrex dish and bake at 350 degrees for 45 to 60 minutes, until done.
9. Cut cake into diamond-shaped servings.
10. Saturate with sugar syrup (recipe follows).

Sugar Syrup

3   cups raw sugar
3   cups water
Juice from 1 or 2 lemons

1. Boil all three ingredients over medium heat for 6 to 8 minutes.
2. Pour over cake and allow to soak in. (You can see why this is used only on special occasions!)

I like this dessert because it's not too sweet. I often omit the citron.

vincenzo's ricotta pie

1½ lbs. ricotta cheese
1   cup raw sugar
1½ cups milk
10 eggs
1   large lemon
1   orange
1   tsp. cinnamon
2   tbsp. brandy or rum
4   tbsp. candied citron

1. Blend ricotta cheese and sugar in a bowl.

2. Add milk and stir to make a smooth, creamy liquid.
3. Beat eggs separately and fold into cheese mixture.
4. Grate lemon and orange skin and add.
5. Add 1 tsp. cinnamon, 2 tbsp. rum or brandy and citron.
6. Place in buttered baking pan that has edges about 2 inches high.
7. Bake in pre-heated 450 degree oven for 1/2 hour.
8. Reduce heat to 300 degrees and cook for another 3/4 hour.

My husband's Aunt Florrie is a gourmet cook who loves to feed people. The only trouble is that by the time you've finished the hors d'oeuvres, you have no room for the rest of the dinner. Every time she visits, she brings Marty his favorite cookies in a coffee tin.

aunt florrie's currant cookies

1   cup butter
1½ cups sugar
2   eggs
2   tbsp. cognac
3½ cups flour
1½ tsp. nutmeg
1/2 cup currants

1. Cream butter and sugar until light and fluffy.
2. Beat in eggs one at a time.
3. Stir in cognac.
4. Sift flour.

5. Add nutmeg and currants to flour and mix.
6. Mix flour with the egg mixture and wrap in waxed paper.
7. Chill dough for several hours or overnight.
8. Roll out dough to a thickness of 1/4 inch.
9. Cut with a cookie cutter and place on lightly greased cookie sheet.
10. Bake at 350 degrees until the edges are slightly browned while the center remains pale. Then cool on rack.

You can't seem to find a good old fashioned coffeecake in the supermarket that doesn't have some kind of preservative, additive, or artificial coloring. Many have all three. So, here is one you can make.

mrs. knudson's coffeecake

1/2 cup butter
1/2 cup shortening
1¼ cups raw sugar
2   beaten eggs
1   cup sour cream
1   tsp. vanilla
2½ cups flour
1   tsp. baking powder
1/2 tsp. baking soda

1.   Preheat oven to 350 degrees.
2.   Cream butter, shortening, and sugar.

3.   Add eggs, sour cream, vanilla and stir.
4.   Sift dry ingredients.
5.   Add the dry ingredients a little at a time, stirring after each addition.
6.   Spread half of the batter in a greased, square, Pyrex dish and cover with half the filling (recipe follows).
7.   Add remaining batter.
8.   Bake at 350 degrees for 1/2 hour.
9.   Spread the remaining filling over cake and cook another 30 minutes or until done.

1/2 cup chopped nuts
1/2 cup dates, chopped
2   tbsp. brown sugar
1/2 tsp. cinnamon

Filling

1.   Mix all ingredients well.

I wasn't sure where to put this, but it seemed that it should come in somewhere for a special breakfast treat, guaranteed to entice all children and many sweet-toothed adults. It is a dish that I first had traveling with my children and my first husband back when we were touring the country. We had it in the dining car of the famous Super Chief train as we were whirling from Chicago across the country towards Los Angeles. The cook didn't give me the recipe himself, so this is my approximation; it seems to come close.

super chief french toast

10 slices white bread (Unfortunately, it just doesn't make it with brown bread.)
4 eggs
1/2 cup milk
1/4 cup flour
1/2 tsp. vanilla
1 tsp. sugar
4 tbsp. butter
2 cups fruit, sliced
Maple syrup

1. Spread bread out on a table for at least 1/2 hour, so that it gets slightly stale.
2. Separate the eggs and beat yolks until frothy.
3. To the yolks, slowly add the milk and flour alternately, making a smooth mixture.
4. Add vanilla and sugar and stir.
5. Beat the egg whites until stiff and fold them carefully into egg yolk mixture.
6. Heat butter in a large frying pan.
7. Dip bread slices into batter making sure to coat both sides.
8. When butter sizzles, fry bread in it until golden brown on each side.
9. Serve with sliced fruit (bananas, apples, strawberries, peaches, etc.) and maple syrup.

my apple crunch

6 cups of tart apples, peeled and sliced
1/4 cup water
1/2 cup sugar
1/2 cup brown sugar
1/4 tsp salt
1/2 tsp. fresh nutmeg, grated
1/2 tsp. cinnamon
3/4 cup flour
1/2 cup butter

1. Place apple slices in a shallow baking dish and sprinkle with the water.
2. Sift all dry ingredients.
3. Cut butter into dry mixture with a pastry fork.
4. Cover apples with this mixture; do not mix.
5. Bake, covered, at 350° for 1/2 hour.
6. Uncover and bake for another 1/2 hour.
7. Serve plain or with ice cream or heavy cream.

Except for chocolate chip cookies and Aunt Florrie's cookies, these are the only other ones I ever eat. The recipe comes from an old and dear family friend, Sally Maruscak, godmother to my daughter, Liza, who lives in my hometown of Roscoe, N.Y. These are wonderful for kids, but then kids like all cookies.

sally's sugar cookies

1   cup butter
1½ cups raw sugar
3   eggs
1   tsp. vanilla
3½ cups sifted flour
2   tsp. cream of tartar
1   tsp. baking powder
1/2 tsp. salt
1/2 cup jam

1. Cream butter and sugar.
2. Add eggs, one at a time, beating after each addition.
3. Stir in vanilla.
4. Sift dry ingredients.
5. Add dry ingredients to egg mixture and blend well.
6. Chill 3 to 4 hours.
7. Roll out dough on well floured board to a thickness of 1/4 inch.
8. Using a round cookie cutter, cut all the dough into circles.
9. Remove a tiny circle from the center of half these circles. (I use something like a bottle cap to cut it out.)
10. Bake all the circles on an ungreased cookie sheet at 375 degrees for 6 to 8 minutes.
11. Cool.
12. Place a dab of jam on each plain circle and top with the cutout version. What you have is a cookie sandwich with a jam filling.

odds
and ends

odds and ends

These are things that are nice to make and very easy. Many people put off preparing them because they think otherwise.

If the mayonnaise doesn't get thick you have poured the oil in too quickly. Once you get the timing right, it's hard to go back to using store-bought mayonnaise because this is so much better. You can also experiment with using different kinds of oil, vinegar instead of lemon juice, more or less mustard, and adding spices, and other ingredients like Tabasco or Worcestershire Sauce.

mayonnaise

2 egg yolks
4 tbsp. lemon juice
1/2 tsp. salt
1/2 tsp. dry mustard
1 cup safflower oil

1. Mix all ingredients, except oil, in a blender.
2. Then blend in the oil very, very slowly until the mayonnaise is thick and creamy.

Sprout seeds can be purchased in health food stores or some gourmet shops. You can use mung beans, alfalfa seeds, soy beans, etc. Again, this is not a complicated process, nor does it take much time, once you get the hang of it.

sprouts

Sprouting seeds
1 quart jar
1 square of cheesecloth
1 rubber band
Water

1. Fill quart jar about 1/5 full with seeds.
2. Fill jar to top with lukewarm water, and let stand in a dark place overnight.
3. In the morning, place cheesecloth over mouth of jar and secure with the rubber band.
4. Gently pour water out of the jar.
5. Add enough lukewarm water through the cheesecloth to rinse sprouts and then gently pour the water out again.
6. Lay jar on its side in a darkened place and repeat this process three times a day until the seeds have sprouted to about a 1-inch length.
7. Keep sprouts in refrigerator for use in salads, Chinese foods, sandwiches, casseroles, etc.

So many recipes call for either chicken or beef broth, and I have yet to find any in the local supermarkets, either in cans or cubes, that do not contain preservatives. Therefore, I make my own broths very simply and freeze them in batches. I also put some in ice cube trays. Sometimes a recipe calls for only 2 tablespoons of broth and these cubes are very handy.

chicken broth

1   package of chicken backs or any other inexpensive cut of chicken.
1/2 tsp. salt
1/4 tsp. pepper
2   tbsp. vinegar
1   small onion, sliced
1   stalk celery, sliced
1   carrot, sliced
6   cups water

1. Wash the chicken parts and place in a two-quart saucepan.
2. Add remaining ingredients and simmer for about an hour or until you have a nice, rich broth.
3. Strain, reserving meat from bones to be used for chicken salad, a casserole, etc.
4. Cool broth and pour into containers; store in freezer.

beef broth

A couple of soup bones or marrow bones
A small package of soup or stew meat
1/2 tsp. salt
1/4 tsp. pepper
1   onion, sliced
6   cups water

1. Put all ingredients in a 2-quart saucepan and simmer for 1½ hours, or until meat is tender, skimming off scum when it first collects on the surface.
2. Drain, reserving the meat for sandwich spreads, barbecues, etc.
3. Cool broth, pour in containers, and store in freezer until needed.

This is a simple, tasty, foolproof marinade to use for fish. I had it many years ago, prepared by the actress Janet Ward, an excellent cook. It's best with a subtle fish, like flounder, sole, or weakfish.

janet's soy marinade

1/2 cup soy sauce
1/4 cup honey
1   tbsp. Worcestershire Sauce
2   cloves garlic
1   tbsp. fresh ginger, grated
1   tbsp. dry mustard
1   tbsp. dry sherry (optional)

1.   Combine all ingredients and mix well.
2.   Use this as a marinade for fish, a sauce to bake it in, or for basting, if the fish is broiled.

This is a nice, simple, French dressing which comes from my Aunt Ruth. She gave it to me many years ago when I was growing up, and I still use it. My aunt never liked to fuss too much in the kitchen, preferring to sit outside and watch the wild deer come down to drink at the pond in her back yard. But whatever she cooked had to be good. Today I omit the sugar. It tastes much the same.

aunt ruth's french dressing

1   clove garlic
2   tsp. dry mustard
1   tbsp. sugar
1/2 tbsp. salt
1   tsp. paprika
1/2 tsp. pepper
1   cup wine vinegar
2   cups safflower oil

1.   Mix all ingredients in a glass jar with a tight-fitting lid.
2.   Store in refrigerator to have on hand whenever you need it.

This is a sauce that I made up to use in place of some preservative-laced brand names sometimes called for in recipes It can also be used on ham, chicken or for sandwiches.

mustard sauce

1¾ tsp. dry mustard
3   tsp. apple cider vinegar
3   tsp. brown sugar
1/2 cup yogurt

1. Mix the dry mustard with the vinegar.
2. Add brown sugar and make a smooth paste.
3. Stir in yogurt and refrigerate until ready to use.

This final recipe comes from Donald Kennedy. It was the most recent of my collection and it seemed like a good one to include because tofu is both nutritious and economical. It also seems to me that more and more food stores are carrying it.

tofu roquefort salad dressing

4   oz. tofu
4   oz. good Roquefort cheese
1/4 cup olive oil
1   tbsp. wine vinegar
1/4 tsp. salt

1. Put tofu and cheese in a blender and slowly pour in olive oil while blending.
2. Add vinegar and salt and stir.

conclusion

This book has been fun for me to write. A lot of my friends whose recipes are included are anxious to see their dishes in print, and to try the concoctions of others. My daughter said to me recently, "Not many kids get the chance to have their mother's cookbook right before them." As I said in the beginning, I like to share recipes, and there is a bonus I had not counted on. Lots of new recipes are being passed on to me by friends and strangers who know what I have been doing. So, I am happily collecting more and more to add to my already overflowing files and, who knows, I may even get enough to start on another book.

Judith Shepard

index

Mail Order Forms

FOOD OF MY FRIENDS

The Permanent Press
Sagaponack, N.Y. 11962

Please send me _____ copies of *Food of My Friends* at $8.95
each. Enclosed is my check or money order for $ _____ ,
made payable to The Permanent Press.

Name _____
       Please Print

Street _____

City _____ State _____ Zip _____

FOOD OF MY FRIENDS

The Permanent Press
Sagaponack, N.Y. 11962

Please send me _____ copies of *Food of My Friends* at $8.95
each. Enclosed is my check or money order for $ _____ ,
made payable to The Permanent Press.

Name _____
       Please Print

Street _____

City _____ State _____ Zip _____

FOOD OF MY FRIENDS

The Permanent Press
Sagaponack, N.Y. 11962

Please send me _____ copies of *Food of My Friends* at $8.95
each. Enclosed is my check or money order for $ _____ ,
made payable to The Permanent Press.

Name _____
       Please Print

Street _____

City _____ State _____ Zip _____